Wills and Probate

Wills and Probate

 CONSUMERS' ASSOCIATION

Which? Books are commissioned and researched by
Consumers' Association and published by
Which? Ltd, 2 Marylebone Road, London NW1 4DF
Email address: books@which.net

Distributed by The Penguin Group:
Penguin Books Ltd, 80 Strand, London WC2R 0RL

First edition 1967
Many new editions including 1988, 1991, 1994, 1995, 1997, 1998, 1999, 2001
Reprinted 2003

British Library Cataloguing in Publication Data
A catalogue record for this book is available from the British Library

ISBN 0 85202 858 X

For a full list of *Which?* books, please write to Which? Books, Castlemead, Gascoyne Way,
Hertford X, SG14 1LH or access our web site at www.which.net

Revisions for this edition:
Paul Elmhirst (England and Wales)
Ewan G. Kennedy (Scotland)
Alastair J. Rankin (Northern Ireland)

Editorial and production: Joanna Bregosz, Nithya Rae

Cover and text design by Kysen Creative Consultants

Typeset by Saxon Graphics Ltd, Derby
Printed and bound in England by Clays Ltd, St Ives plc

Contents

Introduction   7

Part One: Wills

  1   Why you should make a will   11

  2   How to make a valid will   27

Part Two: Probate

  3   How to administer the estate   41

  4   First steps for the executor   45

  5   Applying for probate   57

  6   Distributing the estate   85

  7   Intestacy in England and Wales   99

  8   Wills and confirmation in Scotland   111

  9   Wills and probate in Northern Ireland   139

Part Three: Help with queries

  10   Problems with wills   161

  11   Useful information   167

Index   178

Whether you are writing your own will or sorting out someone else's will, please note that it is important to consult a legal adviser if the situation is at all complex.

Introduction

Death is a subject people do not like to think about. Many people defer, until it is too late, making a decision on what is to happen to their possessions and assets when they die, and writing a will.

This book is intended to help in several ways. First, it looks at wills and explains in simple language the reasons why you should make one. Second, it sets out the various steps in the administration of an estate – probate – both where a will is present and where the person has not left one (i.e. he or she has died intestate). Third, the book touches on the problems which can arise over wills and the administration of estates and suggests solutions.

The Probate Registry provides a service to enable members of the public to administer estates themselves. *Wills and Probate* is aimed at assisting such people, but it also identifies situations where DIY probating is not appropriate and where the sensible reader should consider taking legal advice.

It should also be remembered that this book is a guide – it is not a probate reference book (these usually come in several large volumes) and so cannot contain the detailed information required to deal with a complex issue.

Matters such as inheritance tax are complicated in their application although the general principles are straightforward. This book is designed to equip readers with the basic information, as it is often possible to save thousands of pounds of inheritance tax by making a will and following the guidance set out in this guide. If your financial affairs are substantial or complicated the cost of professional advice is usually low in relation to the tax saving achieved.

This book explains the law and procedure in England and Wales and sets out the main differences which apply in Scotland and Northern Ireland.

Part One

Wills

Chapter 1

Why you should make a will

When a person dies, someone has to make funeral arrangements and someone has to sort out what is to happen to the possessions (such as house and car) and assets (such as shares, unit trust holdings, bank and building society deposits).

A person who makes a will – a testator – can determine his or her own funeral arrangements and the future ownership of possessions and assets.

But if a person dies without making a will – 'intestate' – statutory rules set out not only who is to deal with the estate but also who gets what from it. In some cases, it can be assumed that the intestacy provisions may match a person's wishes exactly but often they may not. Without a will, you cannot choose your executors or appoint a guardian for your children. Even if your spouse faces financial hardship, you cannot ensure that he or she gets all your estate, nor can you arrange your affairs in the best way to minimise inheritance tax. In short, the rules of intestacy amount to a legal straitjacket.

What happens if you do not make a will?

When anyone dies intestate, rules set down by Act of Parliament say who is to administer the estate and how it is to be shared by the family. (These rules apply to England and Wales: see Chapter 7. Minor differences from them operate in Scotland and Northern Ireland: see chapters 8 and 9).

The list on page 59 sets out, in order of priority, which members of the family can apply for 'Letters of administration' for an intestate's estate and the chart on page 59 sets out how it must be divided on intestacy.

If your family and financial circumstances are straightforward, it is possible to write your own will saying what you want to happen when you die. If your circumstances are more involved because of family or financial complications, a will is essential and you may need professional advice.

The rest of this chapter explains how different personal circumstances affect the way you should approach making your will.

Married couples

If the joint assets of a married couple do not exceed £125,000 and if there is no will, everything goes to the surviving spouse on the first death. But, if the joint assets exceed £125,000 and the couple have children, the situation is immediately more complicated. In such a case, the surviving spouse receives the first £125,000 together with the personal belongings of the deceased. The rest of the estate is then divided in two. The children share one half of that sum and the other half is held 'on trust' by the administrators as 'trustees' of the estate. Throughout the surviving spouse's lifetime, they must pay him or her the income arising from that half share. On the death of the surviving spouse, the half share is again divided equally between the children. But, if any of the children are under 18 when they become entitled to their share, the trustees must look after their share until they reach 18.

These rules can cause real difficulty. Suppose a husband (it could just as easily be a wife) dies owning a house worth £150,000 and savings worth £200,000 making the total value of the estate £350,000. The widow has only nominal savings and there are three children. Under the intestacy rules, the widow is entitled to the personal belongings and the first £125,000. Of the remaining £225,000 she gets a life interest in

£112,500 and the children share the other £112,500 between them.

If the widow decides to take the house as part of her share, that takes care of the first £125,000 and £25,000 from her share of the surplus. She then has £87,500 of capital left from the estate to do with as she likes in addition to which she will receive interest from the remaining £112,500 of, say, £4,500 per annum.

If the matter had been covered by a will, the husband would probably have decided to leave all his estate to his wife. She could then have made use of the capital as well as the interest.

Cohabitees

If a couple have lived together for many years as husband and wife, you might expect the law to make automatic provision for the surviving partner. It does not. The law does allow the surviving partner to make a claim against the estate – but only if the couple has been together for more than two years.

Contrary to common belief, the term 'common law spouse' has no standing in law. The estate of a person who dies leaving a partner but no will is divided according to the rules of intestacy. If there are children, they share the entire estate. If they do not see eye-to-eye with the surviving partner (who might or might not be the children's parent), a successful claim against the estate by the surviving partner is at the expense of the children. If the claim is contested, the cost of legal proceedings reduces the overall value of the estate.

Children and guardians

Couples with dependent children should give thought to what happens if both parents are killed in a common accident or, if you are a single parent, what happens to the children if you die.

A mother has automatic 'parental responsibility', as does a married father. (An unmarried father must obtain it by written agreement with the mother and this is then registered at the Principal Registry of the Family Division of the High Court. A second route is by a court order at the magistrates' or county court of the district in which the children are living).

Anyone with parental responsibility can, through their will, appoint another person to act as guardian to the children. The appointment does not take effect until after the death of the surviving parent (if the surviving parent, too, has parental responsibility). If both parents die intestate, the issue of guardianship has to be resolved under the provisions of the Children Act 1989.

Equally important is the question of financial support for a guardian. If a person is to be appointed guardian of dependent children, he or she should, of course, be consulted and thought given to the additional living expenses that such an appointment entails. Will the guardian need a bigger house? Is private education being contemplated? What about the general expense of looking after children? Again, if there is no will, the courts must intervene.

Great care should be taken when drafting a will in which payments are to be made to a guardian for the care of dependent children. What is needed is a realistic but flexible scheme which allows for the cost of raising children from the age of, say, five to independence. At the same time, if the children are in their late teens and almost independent when their parents die, it avoids the payment of a large lump sum. For these reasons, unless there is an additional executor to oversee any conflict of interest that may arise, it may be wise to avoid making the executors guardians as well.

Ownership of businesses and farms

Any detailed consideration of the 'gifting' of businesses and farms is beyond the scope of this guide but, if you own a substantial interest in a business or farm, you must give thought to the following questions.

- If the business is owned by you alone and you want it to continue, what happens on your death? Even if the business is to be sold, it is usually advantageous to sell it as a going concern. That means giving specific and sufficiently wide powers to your executors to keep it going until a buyer is found.
- If the business is run as a partnership what happens on your death? Do you have a workable partnership agreement? At the very least, the partners should consider insuring each other's lives in order to provide sufficient money to buy out the share of the deceased partner without putting an additional financial burden on the business.
- If the business is a private limited company, do the memorandum and articles of association of the company determine what happens to your shares on your death? Can they be gifted by will or must they be offered to the surviving shareholders first? Is there agreement on how the shares are to be valued in the event of the death of one of the shareholders?

The incidence of inheritance tax on the business or farm is a complex matter and beyond the scope of this guide. If you own either, at the time you make your will seek advice on inheritance tax mitigation and provision for retirement.

Foreign property and domicile

If you own property or land in another country, the laws of that country are likely to determine what happens to it on your death and the tax consequences. In such circumstances you must make a will in that country to dispose of your property on your death. Remember not to cancel it accidentally when making your UK will.

If your domicile is in another country but you have assets in England or Wales, you have to obtain a UK grant of representation (probate) to deal with the UK property. Special rules apply where the deceased was domiciled in Scotland or Northern Ireland and, under the Colonial Probate Acts, where your domicile is England or Wales and you have property in the old colonies. Specialist advice should be taken in these cases.

Houses in joint ownership

If a house is owned by one person, he or she can dispose of it as wished through a will. The one exception is where there are other occupants with rights of occupation. In this case, the will must take account of their interests.

Joint ownership of a house can be set up in one of two ways; you can choose to be joint tenants or tenants in common:

- *joint tenants* means that on the death of one joint owner, the deceased person's share passes automatically to the survivor. It is usual, but not essential, for married couples' homes to be held as joint tenants. *Note* that such an arrangement bypasses the provisions of a will or intestacy.
- *tenants in common* means that, on the death of one joint owner, their share passes according to their will or intestacy. If agreement cannot be reached for the surviving tenant in common to buy out the share of the deceased tenant, the property has to be sold and the proceeds divided between the survivor and the estate of the deceased.

Even when the owners are joint tenants, the estate of one of them does not escape inheritance tax, except where the value of the deceased's estate is below the inheritance tax threshold or unless the other joint holder is the surviving spouse. In this case the automatic transfer is exempt from inheritance tax. *Note*, however, that unless special arrangements are made –

for example a discretionary trust (see page 24) – the surviving joint tenant remains liable for inheritance tax on the share of the property which passes to them on the death of their co-owner.

Mortgages and debts

The general rule is that inheritance tax and general debts are paid from the 'residue' of the estate but, if a specific asset is given, any charge or mortgage on it becomes the responsibility of the person who receives the asset. (The 'residue' is the remaining value of the estate after all bequests and debts have been paid).

For example, if a house, which is subject to a mortgage, is given by will without any provision for the mortgage to be repaid from the residue, the person receiving it is responsible for the repayment of the mortgage. He or she must take on the mortgage (or arrange a replacement) or sell the house and repay the mortgage.

Remember, too, that your will should deal with your secured debts and, so there are no misunderstandings, should say how repayment is to be made. This is particularly important when a house is mortgaged with an endowment policy linked to it to repay the debt at the end of the mortgage term. If you want the proceeds of the endowment policy to go to the person who gets the house (subject to the mortgage debt), you must say so in your will.

Debts

If you have debts, you should consider their effect on the value of the residue of your estate. If these are substantial and you have also made specific bequests, the residuary beneficiaries may get much less than you intended. Always take note of the order in which debts must be paid.

Legacies

A legacy or specific bequest is usually made free from inheritance tax but, in certain circumstances where inheritance tax is payable on an estate, it is important to be aware of the financial consequences of a tax-free legacy. For example, take a man who leaves the bulk of his estate to his widow but wants to make a specific legacy of money to his son. If he does this without saying that the legacy is to bear its own tax, the estate has to pay the tax. If the nil rate band has been used up (over £242,000*), the effect is to reduce the amount left to the widow.

Inheritance tax

This was established by the Finance Act 1986. It replaced Capital Transfer Tax (which, in the 1970s, replaced Estate Duty).

Inheritance tax is charged on substantial assets which are bequeathed on death or which have been transferred in the seven years before the death. This period is longer, however, if the deceased continued to receive a benefit from a gifted property such as rent-free occupation.

The tax is imposed on those who were domiciled in the UK at the date of their death. The first £242,000 of an estate is treated as the 'nil rate' band and no tax is due on it. After this tax threshold, inheritance tax is charged on the remainder of the estate at the single rate of 40 per cent. However, if the deceased has been entitled to income from a trust during his lifetime or if he has made any gifts in the seven years before his death, the value of the trust and of any gifts have to be added to the value of the estate.

Tax is then apportioned between the trust on the one hand and the estate, including any gifts, on the other in proportion

---

* This *Guide* assumes the 2001–2 nil rate band: £242,000. The figure is commonly but not always increased in the spring Budget.

to their capital values. The nil rate band is set first against the gifts in the order in which they were made.

For example, if a person died with assets of £200,000, made a gift of £106,000 three years before his or her death and enjoyed the interest from a trust whose capital value was £100,000, the inheritance tax payable is calculated as follows:

Value of the lifetime gift made within the last 7 years		£106,000
Less annual gift allowance plus previous year's allowance (see below)	6,000	
Less part of nil rate band of £242,000	100,000	£106,000
		no tax to pay
Value of the estate		£200,000
Value of the trust		£100,000
		£300,000
Less balance of nil rate band of £242,000		£142,000
Value of estate and trust subject to tax		£158,000
Inheritance tax on £158,000 @ 40% = £63,200		
Tax on estate 200/300 x 63,200 =	42,133	
Tax on trust 100/300 x 63,200 =	21,067	63,200

So, in this case, the post-tax value of the estate available for distribution in accordance with the will is £157,867. The value of the trust is now £78,933. If the lifetime gift had exceeded £242,000 and the death had taken place within the seven years period, inheritance tax would be charged on the gift. In such a case, 'taper relief' is allowed to reduce the tax charged on the gift. Seek advice from the Inland Revenue if you need details of this scheme.

Reducing inheritance tax

There are the following exemptions and reliefs which can mitigate the effect of inheritance tax:

* *annual exemption* – gifts up to a total value of £3,000.
  A gift or gifts up to this amount in total can be made each year free from any inheritance tax. The previous year's

unused allowance of £3,000 can also be brought forward to the current year but it can only be used when the current year's allowance has already been used.

- *small gifts* – this permits any number of tax-free gifts of under £250 each year to different people.
- *normal expenditure* – this permits tax-free gifts from income, providing the gifts can be made within the range of the giver's normal income and expenditure.
- *marriage* – a gift of £5,000 by each parent to children on their marriage, £2,500 by each grandparent to grandchildren on their marriage and £1,000 for another marriage
- *charitable donations* – wholly exempt
- *political donations* – wholly exempt (if to approved political parties)
- *gifts* by husband to wife or vice versa – wholly exempt, provided both are domiciled in the United Kingdom
- *funeral expenses* can be offset against the value of the estate but otherwise only debts existing before the death can be offset against the value of the estate.
- *business property* and *agricultural property* –100 per cent relief is available for the transfer of owner-occupied farms and unincorporated businesses as well as certain other business assets. There is 50 per cent relief available for the interest of landlords in let farmland and in certain business assets. The rules in this area are complicated and, if you are potentially eligible, you should seek legal or accountancy advice.
- *woodlands* – 50 per cent relief is available for managed woodlands. Until the timber is sold, the value of non-commercial woodlands can be left out of inheritance tax calculations and the tax deferred.
- *heritage property* – with the approval of the Inland Revenue, architecturally or historically significant buildings can be designated 'Heritage Property' and are then exempt from inheritance tax. There are conditions attached in such cases, usually relating to public access.
- *quick succession relief*.

Other aspects of inheritance tax

- *time of payment* – inheritance tax is due to be paid within six months of the end of the month in which the death occurred. If not, interest is added. Cases do happen where probate is delayed for a variety of reasons, but the interest is never waived.
- *payment by instalments* – if inheritance tax is payable on the value of land or a property which has not been sold, an election can be made to pay the inheritance tax by equal annual instalments over 10 years. Unless the land is agricultural, interest is charged on the outstanding inheritance tax.
- *alteration of valuations* – it is often necessary to make adjustments to the value of the estate when previously unknown assets or liabilities come to light during the administration. Before completing the administration, these must be disclosed to the Inland Revenue Capital Taxes Office, so a revised inheritance tax assessment can be made. This may lead, in some cases, to a refund to the estate which can be distributed to the residuary beneficiaries.

Other concessions affect the taxable valuation of particular items. For example, if shares are sold within 12 months of the death for less than the probate value, an application can be made by personal representatives or beneficiaries to substitute the lower sale value for the probate value. Similarly, in cases where land or an interest in land is sold within four years from the date of death, it may be possible to substitute the lower sale price for the probate valuation.

Burial, cremation or medical research

These matters are covered in detail in *What to do when someone dies.** If any particular arrangements are required – your

---

* Available from Which? Books, Castlemead, Gascoyne Way, Hertford X, SG14 1LH, or www.which.net

wishes for burial in a particular plot or for your ashes to be scattered in a particular place – they should be set out in the will. If you want to leave your body for medical research or donate your organs for transplantation, you should make arrangements first with your chosen medical school or hospital. These organisations will provide the necessary documentation and a contact address for your executors. It is always wise to tell your executors of the arrangements, so they can act quickly in the event of your death.

Alternative methods of giving

The disposal or gifting of assets by will takes effect on the death of the testator. As the lawyers put it 'The will speaks from the death' – even when probate is delayed. A person can dispose of any asset during their lifetime by outright gift or by creating a trust.

Although professional advice is needed for individual detailed inheritance tax planning, the key points set out below should enable you to consider other possibilities for the disposal of assets, which can be used in conjunction with your will.

Gifts

A lifetime gift can be made to a spouse without inheritance tax or capital gains tax problems, because such gifts to spouses are exempt. A lifetime gift of your own house can similarly be made without incurring capital gains tax because your dwelling house is exempt. If the gift is made to someone other than your spouse, it becomes a PET (a potentially exempt transfer), the value of which, if you die within seven years of making the gift, is added back to the value of your estate for calculating inheritance tax. After seven years, in most circumstances the gift is free of inheritance tax.

The interaction between potential inheritance tax and capital gains tax needs to be watched carefully when making lifetime gifts. Nevertheless, if the person making the gift can divest themselves of assets in this way, a lifetime gift can save large amounts of tax. But the gift is ineffective for tax purposes if the person making it retains an interest in the property. For example, if the donor retains the right to remain there rent-free for the rest of their life, the gift is valid but it does not count as a PET. As a result, when the donor dies, the value of the gifted property is added to the value of the rest of their estate to calculate the total amount of inheritance tax due.

Trusts

A trust can be created by will or lifetime gift. In the latter case, the terms of the trust are set out in the trust document and the trust begins on a chosen date. In the case of a trust created by will, the trust begins on the date of the testator's death.

Remember that a trust puts the legal ownership of property into the hands of and under the control of trustees. Acting on behalf of the beneficiaries of the trust and on the terms set out in the will or deed creating the trust, they are totally responsible for the administration of the property.

So, if you are creating a trust by deed or by will, you must think carefully about the choice of trustees and any replacement. You must also think carefully about the powers to be given to the trustees and the duties imposed on them. Perhaps most important of all, as each type of trust has its own taxation consequences, you must be aware of those that relate to the trust you have decided to establish. A number of trusts can be created by a lifetime gift of assets or money without reservation, which then becomes a PET.

Although no set wording is required to create a trust, the words used must make clear the intentions of the person creating the trust, what the subject matter of the trust is and who the beneficiaries are. To protect the interests of beneficiaries, the powers and obligations of trustees have, over the years, been carefully defined by the law in order to protect the interests of the beneficiaries.

Fixed trusts

These trusts set out, in fixed proportions, who gets what. Some flexibility can be introduced by giving the trustees wider powers but the main advantage of such trusts is their simplicity. They are easy to understand and relatively easy to administer.

Discretionary trusts

These set out who the beneficiaries may be (e.g. wife, children and grandchildren) but then give the trustees the discretion to decide what proportion of income and capital each beneficiary should receive each year. They do not have to pay anything out if they choose not to. Although the person creating the trust, the 'settlor,' can tell the trustees how he or she would like them to exercise their discretion, they are not legally bound by those wishes. The benefit of these trusts is their flexibility.

Accumulation and maintenance trusts

These trusts are usually established to benefit children and grandchildren. Tax concessions are available for these trusts but care must be taken not to extend the period of accumulation beyond the 25th birthday of the beneficiary or the tax concessions are lost. The tax regime applying to accumulation or maintenance trusts is more complicated than in other trusts, so professional advice should be taken.

Protective trusts

These trusts are used to provide for beneficiaries who may be profligate or are liable to be made bankrupt. Frequently the beneficiary receives the income from the trust but the payment of capital may be subject to the discretion of the trustees.

Trusts for disabled beneficiaries

Special arrangements are permitted under the provisions of Section 89 of the Inheritance Tax Act 1984 giving favourable tax treatment to what are, in essence, discretionary trusts.

Taxation of trusts

The taxation of trusts is a subject in itself. If you are contemplating the creation of a lifetime trust, you should seek advice on both inheritance tax and capital gains tax consequences. You should also investigate the income tax consequences of creating such a trust.

Can a will be changed after the testator's death?

Many people find it difficult to settle their wills because the future is uncertain and they do not have a crystal ball to predict the circumstances of their family at the time of their death. No doubt a number of people die intestate because of their indecision over these problems.

Fortunately, as the law stands at present, there is a way out. Under the Inheritance Tax Act 1984, if all the beneficiaries agree to the variation, a will may be varied or the intestacy provisions altered and treated as having been made by the deceased. Such a variation must be made within two years of a death and written notice of the variation given to the Capital Taxes Office within six months of the variation.

If an existing beneficiary is under 18, he or she cannot legally relinquish a benefit (if a variation involved reducing a child's interest, an application would have to be made to the court for approval). The variation can be useful where, for instance, a person dies leaving the whole of his or her estate of, say, £300,000 to his or her spouse (involving no inheritance tax because of the surviving spouse exemption). However, if the surviving spouse dies within two years of the first death, the variation can be used to use the £242,000 nil rate tax band on the first death leaving only £58,000 to add to the estate of the second to die.

Although the use of post-death variations appears to contravene the doctrine established by case law whereby the

Inland Revenue can disallow a scheme devised purely to avoid tax, it continues to allow the use of post-death variations at least in straightforward cases. Remember that, rather than relying on your heirs to vary your will when you are dead, it is still best to make a well thought-out will and to consider possible alterations on a regular basis.

A disclaimer can also be used to produce a similar result to a post-death variation of the will or intestacy but it is less flexible. Providing a beneficiary has taken no 'enjoyment' (that is, has not benefited) from property left in a will, he or she can disclaim the benefit within two years of the death. In this case the property goes to the next person entitled as though the gift had been made to the replacement beneficiary by the testator in the first place. A disclaimed legacy goes to the residuary beneficiaries but a disclaimed share of the residue may pass to the other beneficiaries or, if there are none, it may pass according to the rules of intestacy.

Chapter 2

How to make a valid will

Your first question should be: 'Do I make the will myself or pay someone to do it for me'? There is no simple answer. Some people always want to write their own will* because they like to do their own thing or save money. Others always want to instruct someone else because they do not want to risk getting it wrong.

If your estate is unlikely to be liable for inheritance tax and if your wishes and circumstances are straightforward, you should have no difficulty in preparing and completing your own will. In other cases, matters may be complicated by a range of factors – for example, inheritance tax, divorce, the presence of trusts, the ownership of businesses or your particular wishes for the disposal of your estate. In this case, even if you prepare the draft will yourself, it is sensible to discuss it in draft form with a solicitor first before signing the final version.

Whether you make the will yourself or instruct others, the principles are the same. If you do it yourself, the golden rule is to keep it simple and avoid ambiguity.

The first step – a check list

As a first step, make a list of your assets and liabilities as well as any other points which you wish to cover in your will. These are the common and important matters you must bear in mind:

---

* See *Make Your Own Will* (Which? Books).

- *the beneficiaries* – who are they? Are any under 18? If so, do you want to give the executors power to release money to them before they reach 18 (or 21)?
- *divorce or marriage* – are either of these steps anticipated for you or any beneficiary?
- *foreign property* – do you own any? If so, you should make a will in that country to deal with it. If you have already done so, do not negate that will accidentally by using the normal revocation clause in your UK will.
- *executors* – do you know who they will be? Are they willing to act for you? Are they younger than you?
- *guardians* – if you have infant children and you die, who looks after them? Would your chosen guardian have enough money to care for them as you would like?
- *trusts* – are there any existing trusts which might affect inheritance tax on your estate? In any case, it may be sensible to create a trust yourself through your will.
- *gifts* – have you made any gifts in your lifetime which qualify as 'PETs' (potentially exempt transfers)? Have you made any gifts which do not qualify as PETs because you have retained an interest or benefit?
- *inheritance tax* – if your estate is likely to be subject to inheritance tax, is there any way to avoid or reduce it?
- *claims* against your estate – is there a chance of any claims being made if you leave someone out? Should you include an explanation for any exclusion?
- *automatic change of property* – what property automatically changes hands irrespective of what your will says. For example, do you own your house as a joint tenant? Do you have insurance policies written in trust for your spouse and children?
- *specific items* – are there any you want to leave to a particular person?
- *specific sums of money* – are there any you want to leave to a particular person?
- *residue* of your estate – what do you want to happen to it?
- *your body* – do you have any specific wishes? Do you want it buried, cremated or given for medical research?
- *pet animals* – if you have any, what is to happen to them?

Once you have considered answers to all the relevant points, you can start to write your will. Use simple language and avoid any expressions which are vague or ambiguous or which you do not fully understand.

How to set out the will

There is no single way to set out a will but the following guidelines may be helpful:

- *starting the will* – put in your full name (including any aliases) and your address. You can also include the date in this paragraph.
- *revocation* – you should revoke earlier wills in order to avoid ambiguity. Remember, if you have made a foreign will to dispose of foreign property, you must specifically exclude it from your revocation.
- *marriage* – if you are going to be married, you should state that the will is made 'in contemplation of marriage'. If you do not, the marriage automatically revokes the will.
- *appoint your executors* – always appoint at least two executors, so the death of one still leaves one in place. You may also wish to appoint substitutes in case both your appointed trustees die before you or if they decline to act. It is common practice, if you are creating a trust for, say, infant children, to make your executors your trustees as well.
- *guardians* – if you are appointing guardians of your infant children, make any necessary financial provision for them to cover the cost of looking after your children.
- *specific gifts* – if you have any particular items to give, describe them clearly. For example, say: 'The painting of Sunflowers by Van Gogh' rather than 'The painting on my sitting room wall that my niece likes'. Remember that if you dispose of the item before your death, the beneficiary gets nothing.

- *legacies* – always give a fixed amount. If the beneficiary dies before you, the legacy lapses unless an alternative recipient is set out in your will. A different rule applies if the beneficiary is your child or other descendant. In such a case, if your child died before you, leaving children of his or her own (your grandchildren), they would share what their parent would have received.
- *residue* – this is what is left after all debts, expenses and legacies have been paid. The wording can take a very simple form such as 'I leave everything else I own to my wife Susan, subject only to the payment of all my debts and testamentary expenses'. The traditional way is to give the residue to the executors as trustees on 'trust for sale' with power to postpone the sale. Although the legal need to impose a trust for sale on the residue is debatable, the traditional form of words is still effective: 'my trustees shall hold the rest of my estate on trust for sale on the following terms:....'

You then set out in order what happens to the residue. For example, the will might say that you direct your executors to:

- pay my debts, funeral expenses and inheritance tax on all property passing under my will
- pay the residue to my wife
- if my wife predeceases me, pay the residue to the following persons in the proportions stated:

  1. to John Brown a one half share
  2. to Lois Johnson a one quarter share
  3. to Sophie Oakland a one quarter share

What powers do the trustees have?

The law provides automatic powers for the trustees of your will to enable them to carry out their duties. The main ones are:

- *the power of advancement* – allows trustees to advance capital to an infant beneficiary who has not yet reached the age when he or she becomes absolutely entitled. The advancement is limited to one half of the beneficiary's expected share.
- *the powers of appropriation* – enables the trustees to pass over shares or property in order to satisfy a legacy or bequest
- *the power to run the testator's business* – enables the trustees, while they try to sell the business as a going concern, to run it for up to a year.
- *the power of trustees to charge* – under the Trustee Act 2000, 'Trust Corporations' and professional trustees may charge for work done, even where the will does not contain a charging clause. Generally speaking a trustee cannot charge for work done as trustee but can recover expenses.
- *the power to delegate* – trustees may delegate their administrative powers but not their powers of distribution. A recent change in the law (the Trustee Act 2000) has greatly expanded and clarified the position.
- *insurance* –the trustees have power to insure trust property.
- *investment* – while the Trustee Act 2000 gives wide powers of investment to the trustees, it also places them under a duty to obtain and consider proper investment advice and to review their investments each year. The advisor must be suitably qualified, with appropriate expertise and subject to a professional code of conduct. In your particular circumstances, you may feel that further powers are needed by your trustees including the extension of some of the statutory powers.

The following additional trustee powers are often found in wills:

- *the power to postpone* the sale of property held on trust.
- *the power to advance* all the capital to benefit a beneficiary in satisfaction of their 'contingent' interest – for example, where someone is entitled to payment when they reach 21,

31

this power enables the trustees to make the payment at any time from age 18 onwards.

- *wide powers of investment* including the right to invest in non-income producing assets such as insurance policies.
- *the specific power* to carry on your business beyond the first year.
- *additional power to borrow.*
- *the power to use income or capital* to improve trust property.
- *the power to sell assets* to beneficiaries who are also trustees.
- *making a declaration* – your will can include 'declarations' giving specific instructions to your executors to ensure they follow your wishes exactly. For example, you can state that references to 'children' in your will should always include stepchildren.

Some typical declarations are set out below:

- *advance payments* – you can state: 'if any beneficiary in my will has received an advance payment from me, no account of that advance shall be taken when ascertaining the entitlement of that beneficiary'. Or conversely: 'if any beneficiary in my will has received an advance from me, that advance shall be taken into account with/without interest when ascertaining the entitlement of that beneficiary'.
- *foreign property* – if you have made a foreign will disposing of foreign property, make clear in your UK will what property is covered by the foreign will.
- *funeral arrangements* – if these are complicated, write that detailed instructions for your funeral have been given to the executors. The will can then state your preference for burial or cremation.
- *donation of your body for medical research* – if you wish to donate your body, contact your chosen medical school or teaching hospital, which can give guidance and information on the best way to make the donation effective.

Essential formalities

If you fail to observe the essential formalities, you may invalidate your will. These points must be followed whenever or however a will is made:

- The will must be in writing – handwritten or typed.
- The will must be signed by you (see below for formalities for those unable to read or write).
- You should sign the will in such a way as to make absolutely clear your intention to give effect to the will. In other words, rather than signing it on the back or on the side of the will, sign it at the end of the writing on the final page.
- Your signature should be made or acknowledged in the presence of two witnesses (who must not be beneficiaries or potential beneficiaries under the will). They must be present at the same time as you sign and must then 'attest' and sign the will themselves. It is also advisable for you and your witnesses to sign the bottom of each page of the will. *Note* that if the will does not have an attestation clause in it, your witnesses will be asked, on your death, to sign an affidavit confirming they were both present when you signed the will. A typical attestation clause might be worded as follows: 'signed by the testator in our presence and attested by us in the presence of the testator and each other'.
- If a testator is blind, the attestation clause says that the will was read to him or her and that, having stated that he understood it, he signed it or, alternatively, it was signed on his behalf. Appropriate variations have to be made for illiterate testators (who cannot read) or for physically handicapped testators (who may not be able to read or write).

Marriage and divorce

Even if the will leaves everything to the person you intend to marry, a will is revoked by marriage. In this case, you must make a new will. The only exception is when your will is made 'in anticipation of marriage' to a particular person in which case the will remains valid.

If you have made a will but are now contemplating divorce, you should note that the granting of a decree absolute or annulment means that your ex-spouse is treated as having died on the date of the decree and loses the benefits given to her by the will although she may still be entitled to make a claim against your estate.

Making a valid will

In order to make a valid will, you must be over 18 (unless you are a soldier on active service) and have 'testamentary capacity'. This means that you understand the nature and effect of the will you are making. It also means that you understand what property you are disposing of and that you are aware of those who might reasonably be expected to benefit under your will. It may occasionally be difficult to distinguish an eccentric testator with testamentary capacity from a conventional testator who lacks testamentary capacity.

Your will must also be the result of your own wishes. If you make a will as a result of being pestered by your children to do so that is acceptable. However, a will favouring someone who brought undue influence on the testator can be declared invalid by the courts.

The only exception to the rule on testamentary capacity is where the person (called the 'patient' and usually mentally ill or incapable) is subject to a Court of Protection order. The court can allow such a will to replace an existing will or where the patient's intestacy might disadvantage the patient's family. In such cases, you should seek legal advice.

Reciprocal or mirror wills

These are common arrangements for married couples who make more or less identical wills. Usually, spouses leave their estate to the other. Where both have died, the estate is divided equally between their children.

Reciprocal or mirror wills should not be confused with a joint or mutual will. This describes a will made by two people incorporating a contractual obligation on the survivor not to change the terms of their own will. Such an arrangement can only be over-ridden by a subsequent marriage. Joint and mutual wills are rare and, other than in exceptional circumstances, are not to be encouraged. They can cause great hardship by preventing the alteration of the survivor's will if circumstances change in an unanticipated way.

Costs of a will

Solicitors charge anything from £50 to £150 or more for preparing a will depending on the complexity and time spent. If your solicitor is asked to advise on inheritance tax mitigation, he or she may call in an investment advisor. Always ask beforehand how much the advisor charges. Remember to add VAT to professional fees. Prepare questions beforehand and aim to get to the point quickly during consultations with professionals who are charging by their time.

Legal Aid

Legal Aid for advice and assistance in making a will is only available to people who fall within the financial limits of the scheme (in receipt of income support, working families tax credit or other means-tested benefits) and within one of the following categories:

- aged 70 or more
- blind, deaf or dumb or suffering from certain other handicaps; or parent of such a person
- single parent caring for a child wishing to make a will appointing a guardian for a child.

Specimen will

This Will dated the [day/month] 2001 is made by me MARY BLAKE of The Firs Willow Lane Minford Surrey

1. I revoke all earlier wills

2. I appoint as my executors and trustees my son ROBERT ANTHONY BLAKE of The Farm Oakburton Devon and my daughter JANE BLAKE of 20 The Close Lower Warton Cumbria

3. I give the following legacies:

   a To DAVID JOHNSON of 18 Tiptree Court Minford the sum of Five hundred pounds (£500)

   b To KATYA KROPOTKIN of 6 Westbury Gardens Far Town South Yorkshire the sum of Five hundred pounds (£500)

   c To the NSPCC the sum of One thousand pounds (£1,000) and I direct that the receipt of a person who appears to be a proper officer of the charity shall be a discharge to my trustees

4. My trustees shall hold the rest of my estate on trust on the following terms: -

   a To pay debts executorship expenses and any inheritance tax in respect of property passing under my Will

   b To divide the residue equally between my son ROBERT ANTHONY BLAKE and my daughter JANE BLAKE but if either of them should die before me leaving children those children shall on attaining eighteen (18) take the share which their parent would otherwise have inherited

5. My trustees shall have the following powers: -

   a To postpone indefinitely the sale of any property held on trust for sale

   b To apply for the benefit of any beneficiary who is under eighteen (18) the whole or any part of the capital to which he is or may become entitled

   c To invest as if they were beneficially entitled which power includes the right to invest in non-income producing assets including insurance policies

6. I express a wish that my body should be cremated

Signed by the Testator
in our presence and
attested by us in the
presence of the testator   _____
and each other   signature of Testator

Witness signature   _____

Full Name   _____

Address   _____

                       _____

                       _____

Occupation   _____

Witness signature   _____

Full Name   _____

Address   _____

                       _____

                       _____

Occupation   _____

Part Two

Probate

Chapter 3

How to administer the estate

In this and the following three chapters you will find out how to deal with the administration. No two estates are exactly the same. What can be explained is the practical routine to follow step by step.

Necessary formalities

First of all, relatives (or friends) have the difficult job of handling the necessary formalities after someone's death. Most people now die in hospital but, even where that does not happen, a doctor must provide the relatives with a certificate giving the cause of death. The certificate is then registered within five days at the Registry of Births, Deaths and Marriages in the district where the death occurred. The registrar needs to know when and where the death took place and personal details of the deceased person, including date of birth, address and, in the case of married women, maiden name. The registrar normally expects to see the birth certificate and marriage certificate of the deceased person. The person who registers the death is called 'the informant', usually a relative who was present at the death or during the illness that preceded death. It can also be the person who is arranging the funeral. If you have questions about who the informant ought to be, telephone the Registrar's Office.

If the doctor says the cause of death is uncertain, arrangements are more complex. The death is first reported to the Coroner, who usually orders a post-mortem. If it shows that the cause of death was natural, the Coroner then authorises the burial or cremation. In such a case, you are issued with a death certificate by the Registrar and a second certificate permitting the undertaker to arrange burial or cremation of the body. That certificate is usually passed to the undertaker.

Except in rare cases, such as violent death when the Coroner orders an inquest to be held, the way is now clear to make the funeral arrangements. *Note* that before you start, it is wise to check the will (if there is one) or, if there is no will, to find out who is responsible for administering the estate.

Arranging the funeral

If there is a will, it may contain the funeral wishes of the deceased.* Even if it does not, it is usually the executors of the will who instruct the undertaker to conduct the funeral and who thus become legally responsible for paying the undertaker. If the executors request a member of the family to organise the funeral, he or she should confirm that the executors are paying for the funeral. The section on debts (see 'Responsibilities and rules', opposite) explains how the funeral costs can be paid by the executors before they have obtained probate of the will.

In a similar way, where the deceased dies intestate, the 'administrators' of an estate who instruct the undertaker become responsible for paying his or her charges from the assets of the estate. Again, it is important to be clear who is going to pay for the funeral before the arrangements are made. This can be particularly important where the deceased has been living with a partner for many years but has not made a will making the surviving partner an executor. In such a case, disagreement may arise between the surviving partner and the executors or the family (in the case of intestacy) as to what the funeral arrangements should be.

---

* *What to do when someone dies* covers funerals in detail and is available from Which? Books, Castlemead, Gascoyne Way, Hertford X, SG14 1LH, or www.which.net

You should also be aware that the provision of a headstone or other memorial is not a funeral or testamentary expense. Before committing expenditure to a memorial, the executors must obtain the consent of the residuary beneficiaries.

In some cases, it may be clear that the deceased does not have enough assets to cover the funeral. If that is the case or if the executors suspect it is, do not instruct the undertaker until you know for certain. Otherwise, you have to pay for the funeral from your own pocket. You can make a claim from the local Benefits Agency but, even if it is successful, the amount of the payment is modest and would not cover the cost of a typical funeral.

Once you know when the funeral is to take place, and especially where the deceased person has been well known, put a notice in the deaths column of one or more newspapers, local and national. This brings the news to relatives and friends who might not otherwise hear of it. Look for the deceased's address book and contact people to tell them of the death.

Responsibilities and rules

Executors and administrators have important responsibilities. They are under a duty to ensure that the assets of the estate are paid to the correct beneficiaries. If the executors distribute the estate to the beneficiaries without having paid all the debts, they may be held personally liable to creditors who cannot recover their money. In order to protect themselves, executors should advertise the death in the *London Gazette* – a newspaper for formal notices of all kinds – and a local paper together with a request that any creditors should submit their claims by a date which must be at least two months after the advertisement. (Although solicitors can place advertisements in the *London Gazette* at an early stage in the administration, private individuals normally have to produce a copy of the probate before their advertisement is accepted for publication).

If you come across a large debt which looks as if it may exceed the value of the assets of the estate, take advice immediately. Special rules govern the order in which certain debts have to be paid. For example, secured creditors such as a building society are always entitled to repayment of the mortgage from the proceeds of sale of the house before beneficiaries receive any share of the residue. After that, the funeral and testamentary expenses have priority, followed by outstanding income tax and VAT.

In some cases, the estate may be sufficiently large to pay off the debts but not large enough to meet all the specific bequests to beneficiaries. If so, the legatees each receive a proportion of their legacy. Those people identified in the will to share the residue get nothing.

Chapter 4

First steps for the executor

Let us now assume you are the executor of a valid will. (If there is no will and you are the administrator, you take on the tasks of arranging the funeral, calling in the assets and paying the debts in the same way. See chapters 7, 8 and 9 for the distribution arrangements in cases of intestacy in different parts of the United Kingdom). You have registered the death and are dealing with the funeral arrangements. You can now begin the process of administering the estate.

Preparing for probate

There are several essential practical steps you need to take before applying for probate. In most cases, you can handle the paperwork yourself. But if you are uncertain what to do – if, for example, there are discretionary trusts to deal with – take legal advice.

Immediate action

The next six items deal with the security of the deceased person's possessions and affairs and are a priority.

Safeguarding the house
If the deceased was living alone, ensure that the house is made safe and that, as far as possible, any valuables are removed from the house for safe-keeping. How this is done depends on the type of property and locality. It is sensible to

give your name and telephone number to a friendly neighbour who may be willing to keep an eye on things. Tell the police that the property is empty and you may wish to obtain advice on security from the police security adviser.

Animals

Make arrangements for any pets. The will may say what should happen to them but executors will probably decide to ask for help from a relative or an animal welfare charity.

Insurance

Check the terms and conditions of the household insurance and notify the insurance company of the death and the fact that the house is empty. Insurance is usually allowed to continue for a month or two on the normal basis but, if the property remains empty for a longer period, you may need to arrange additional cover; for example against damage by vandalism. Similarly, if there is a car or any motor vehicle, the insurance company should be notified of the death. No one should drive the car without first confirming that it is still insured.

Services

You can leave the services on for the time being but, in case of leaks or frost, consider having the gas and water turned off.

Post

Arrange for the post to be redirected to you as executor. Incoming post may provide evidence of assets which might otherwise not be found – for instance, a request for payment of an insurance premium or a notice about changes in interest rates from a building society.

Bank accounts in the deceased's name

Write to the bank as soon as possible to tell them of the death. Apart from funds for funeral expenses, the probate fee, and in some cases inheritance tax, current accounts are frozen at death. Cancel standing orders and variable direct debits. Ask for confirmation of the balance in the account at death and a claim form for you to complete when probate is granted. For interest-bearing and joint accounts see overleaf.

You also need to set up an executor's bank account to receive payments from the deceased's assets and meet liabilities. Consider asking the deceased's own bank or one where you are known. You may need to arrange a bank loan to meet immediate debts and later to pay any inheritance tax due before probate is granted. Interest charged by the bank is paid by the estate.

Establishing the value of the estate

Before you can apply for probate of the will, you have to find out the extent and value of the estate's assets and liabilities. If the deceased was an orderly person, you may find a box or file containing title deeds, share certificates, building society passbooks, insurance policies and a list of any other assets as well as particulars of mortgaged property or hire purchase agreements. Alternatively, you may find that the documents are in drawers, boxes and cupboards spread all over the house. You may find no evidence at all. In such circumstances, you have to become a detective and look for letters or receipts which may give a clue as to the existence of an insurance policy or the name of a bank or a firm of solicitors who may be holding title deeds and other securities. If the deceased was a taxpayer, a good starting point is to approach the local tax office for a copy of his or her last tax return, sending a copy of the will to prove your status as an executor. If you know it, quote the National Insurance number of the deceased.

Once you have discovered an asset, you need to know its value at the date of death. The way you do this depends on the asset and whether it was owned absolutely by the deceased or was jointly owned. You also need to find out the deceased's debts and whether he or she made any lifetime and substantial gifts.

Interest-bearing accounts
Ask for details of any deposit accounts and accrued interest at the time of death. This is needed for the tax return you have to complete on behalf of the deceased's estate.

Joint bank accounts
These can be difficult to deal with. If the joint holders are husband and wife, the account passes automatically to the survivor and the presumption is that the money in the account was held equally by the husband and wife. In other cases, you need to establish the intentions of the joint owners or the contribution of each to the joint account. This is because the amount contributed by the deceased forms part of his or her estate for tax purposes (except where a written agreement confirms that the money in the account passes automatically to the survivor). In the case of a business partnership bank account, you need a set of final trading accounts to the date of death and should contact the surviving partner or partners.

National Savings
These may take the form of National Savings Certificates, National Savings Investment Accounts or Premium Bonds. A claim form for repayment can be obtained from the Post Office and submitted to the appropriate Department for National Savings together with a copy of the probate, when you have it. Always seek confirmation that there are no other assets in the name of the deceased held by National Savings. For example, there may be unclaimed Premium Bond winnings.

Building societies
Building societies should also be approached with requests for the balance of the account plus accrued interest at the date of death. You should ask for a claim form to submit for payment.

Life insurance

Write to each insurance company quoting the date of death and the policy number and enclosing a copy of the death certificate. As with banks and building societies, insurance companies should be asked to provide a claim form and details of the sum to be paid on death. Once probate has been obtained, complete and submit the form. In many cases, policies are held on trust and do not form part of the estate. Insurance companies know this and, on production of the death certificate, make payment direct to the beneficiaries.

Stocks and shares

Give a list of stocks and shares held by the deceased to a stockbroker or bank or, in the case of PEPs and ISAs, the plan manager and ask them for a valuation. The charge for this is usually calculated as a percentage of the total valuation. Ask for transfer forms for all shareholdings.

If you decide to make valuations yourself, you need a copy of the official *Stock Exchange Daily Official List* for the day on which the deceased died. The valuation figure is calculated by adding 25 per cent of the difference between the selling and buying prices. So, if the selling price is 505p and the buying price is 525p, the valuation for probate purposes is 505p plus 25 per cent of 20p – 510p in total. If the death took place at the weekend, you can choose either the Monday or Friday valuation.

However, if the executors sell any shares at a loss within 12 months, the selling price in each case can be taken as the value at the date of death. *Note* that all sales in the 12 months must be included on the same basis. You cannot pick and choose which to include and which to leave out.

If you do not have all the share certificates, you may be able to find dividend counterfoils or tax vouchers among the papers of the deceased which enable you to check the number of shares held in the company. If you cannot find the share certificates, write to the registrar of the company. Names of registrars are given in the Register of Registrars which may be kept at your public library. Alternatively, telephone or write to the company head office. *Note*: if you need a duplicate certificate, you have to sign a letter of indemnity provided by the company.

An increasing number of shares are now held electronically – that is without printed certificates. All you need in this case is a confirmation letter from the nominated stockbroker.

Unit trusts

Like stocks and shares, unit trust valuations are given in the *Stock Exchange Daily Official List.* You can also ask the trust manager for the value on the day in question. Again, a transfer form is needed.

Private companies

In the case of shares in private companies where no value of shares is published, you may sometimes be able to obtain a valuation from the secretary of the company. In the case of a family company, in which the deceased had a significant shareholding, it is usually necessary to have the value determined by an independent accountant.

Pensions

If the deceased was already receiving a pension, you should write to the company operating the pension scheme in order to find out whether the pension is paid up to the date of death. In some cases the pension may have been overpaid in which case a refund has to be made. In other cases, the scheme may make a death benefit. If the deceased had a personal pension fund but had not reached retirement age, a capital sum is repayable by the personal pension provider. This sum may or may not form part of the estate of the deceased. In some cases, it has been written in trust for the surviving spouse and dependants of the deceased and therefore does not form part of the estate.

State benefits

If the deceased was receiving an old age pension, notice of the death should be given to the Department of Work and Pensions, so that adjustments can be made. In the case of a married man, the agency makes arrangements to begin paying widow's pension. It sometimes happens that an elderly person has been claiming means-tested benefits such as income support to which they were not entitled. This can arise when they have deliberately or accidentally failed to inform the agency of the full extent of their income or savings. Check on this before you pay anything out. The agency may seek to recover any overpayment as a debt.

Businesses

The valuation of a business on the death of one of the partners is complicated and depends upon the nature of the business, the way in which the accounts are prepared and the extent of the assets held by the business. You should seek advice from a solicitor or accountant before you try to put a value on the business. The surviving partner/s should make available a set of partnership accounts to the date of death and help you determine the correct valuation for the deceased's share.

Farms

If the deceased owned a farm or a share in a farm, you should seek professional advice from an agricultural valuer as well as a solicitor or accountant. Remember that, although the value of an estate including a farm is usually above the inheritance tax threshold, agricultural relief is available, under certain conditions, to set against any tax liability.

Residential property

If the estate is below the inheritance tax threshold, you may be able to estimate the value of the property by looking at similar properties in estate agent's windows. If the estate reaches the inheritance tax threshold or comes close to it, the figure is checked by the District Valuer. This is the government official instructed by the Inland Revenue to carry out property valuations on its behalf.

If the property is to be retained as an investment or if its value at the date of death is significant, it is advisable to have your own professional valuer who can negotiate the value with the District Valuer. If a property is sold within four years of the death for less than the probate valuation, and providing the sellers are the executors and not beneficiaries, the sale price may be substituted for the original valuation.

Joint properties

Joint owners of properties can either be joint tenants or tenants in common. Married couples normally hold their property as joint tenants which means that, if one of them dies, his or her share passes automatically to the survivor. Where the property is held as tenants in common and one of the owners dies, his or her share passes according to their will or to their next of kin (if they die intestate) rather than to the co-owner of the property.

The value of the share of the person who has died forms part of his or her estate for tax purposes. However, if the share passes to the spouse, the 'surviving spouse exemption' applies. This means that there is no inheritance tax to pay, even if the estate exceeds the inheritance tax threshold.

If it is crucial to keep the value of the estate down for inheritance tax purposes, an argument can be put forward to the District Valuer to discount the value of a half share in a property by 10 or 15 per cent. Again, you may find that, in cases where such a discount would reduce inheritance tax significantly, the cost of engaging a professional valuer pays for itself. (Discounting in this way is not available where the property is jointly owned by spouses).

Mortgaged property

If there is a mortgage on the property at the date of death, the amount of the debt must be found by writing to the bank or building society. The value of the house is reduced by this amount, although both figures appear in the estate's accounts

Where the deceased has bequeathed residential property as a specific item, the will may either say that the property is to be transferred to the beneficiary free from any mortgage or that it is to be subject to the mortgage. The terms of the will should be read carefully to establish which course of action is required and professional advice taken if necessary. The Administration of Estates Act 1925 provides that a person who is bequeathed a mortgaged property is responsible for repaying the mortgage unless the will sets out a contrary intention. *Note* that even if the will contains a provision for the payment of 'debts' from the residue, that does include the repayment of a mortgage. The situation can be even more complicated where there is an insurance policy which either repays the mortgage or passes into the residue of the estate.

Other property and buildings

If the deceased owned commercial property, the executor has to find out if this was a business asset (in which case its value affects the value of the business) or whether it is an investment property unconnected with any business. In that case, it has to be valued separately. Again, if the property is jointly owned, the contribution of each owner has to be established. Professional assistance is essential in such cases.

House contents and other possessions

It is not always necessary to have a professional valuation of household goods (which include motor vehicles and personal possessions). But estimated values are examined more carefully by the District Valuer if the estate is large enough to attract inheritance tax. If there are paintings, furniture or other contents of value, get a professional valuation. In addition to calculating the value of the estate, this can also provide useful proof at a later stage for capital gains tax calculations when assets are sold or to satisfy an insurance company that goods did exist and were of a specific value.

The way in which household assets are dealt with depends on their value. If the value is low, the executor may choose to distribute them among family members. In other cases, the executor may identify a charity willing to take them for sale or distribution to families in need in the locality.

Where the assets have greater value, the executor may wish to take advice from a local auction-house. They can identify any exceptional items to send to a specialist or one of the large international auction houses. Remember that, if there is a dispute among beneficiaries over who should get particular items not specifically mentioned in the will, these can be put into an informal family auction or a public sale. Dissatisfied beneficiaries can then bid against one another for each item. The price the item fetches (less auctioneers' commission) forms part of the assets of the estate.

Cars can be sold at specialist auction or to a garage. They may be taken by a member of the family at a price given in a current car price magazine. The executor signs the logbook and then hands over ownership to the beneficiary or purchaser. As executor, check first to make sure there is no hire purchase debt on the car.

Debts

The debts of the estate as well as the funeral expenses and cost of the headstone can be deducted from the assets to give a net figure. This includes any overpaid pension or income tax due at the date of death as well as hire purchase debts, mortgages and the various utility charges.

Matrimonial liabilities

Some testators leave their spouse or a child out of their will. As executor, remember that claims can be made to the court, so you may need to delay distribution until the legal position is clear. Claimants can also include an ex-spouse receiving maintenance at the time of death.

Income tax

It is unlikely that, before you make your application for probate, you will be in a position to calculate the income tax owing to the date of death. In some cases, it may be possible to make an estimate or to obtain one from the deceased's accountant. Otherwise, you should write to the local tax office quoting the deceased's National Insurance number and requesting a tax return for the period from the previous 6 April up to the date of death. As the administration progresses, you gather the information needed to complete the tax return. If some tax allowances have not been used up, you may find that the estate is entitled to a refund. This is often the case when the old age pension is the only untaxed source of income and any investment income or earnings have been taxed at source. On the other hand, if the deceased was a higher rate taxpayer, there may be additional tax to pay from the estate before distribution.

Lifetime gifts

This can be a tricky matter for an executor who is not familiar with the affairs of the deceased person. The executor is legally obliged to disclose to the Inland Revenue whether the deceased made any gift since March 1986 which exceeded the exempt gift limit (currently £3,000 per person per annum).

This means that an executor cannot safely distribute the estate until he or she is sure that all the inheritance tax arising on lifetime gifts has been paid. If the executor distributes the estate and then finds that he or she cannot recover outstanding tax from the recipient of a lifetime gift, the executor may be personally liable for the shortfall.

Chapter 5

Applying for probate

Probate is official proof of the validity of a will and is granted by the court on production by the executors of the necessary documents. Only when probate is obtained are the executors free to administer and distribute the estate.

When and why probate is needed

If the estate is under £5,000 in total, it may be possible to administer the estate without obtaining probate of the will. If, for instance, the estate consists of a house held in joint ownership as joint tenants and if the only other asset is a small building society account or bank account, the house passes automatically to the survivor. You can then complete a declaration form for the building society or bank undertaking to distribute the estate in accordance with the will or intestacy law but without having to obtain either probate of the will or letters of administration.

Generally, if there are assets, you have to apply for probate of the will or letters of administration. There are several reasons for this:

- Banks, building societies and National Savings are governed by the Administration of Estates (Small Payments) Act 1965. This only allows them to refund individual accounts up to £5,000 without production of probate.

- You cannot sell stocks, shares or land from the estate without probate, except in the case of land where it is held as joint tenants as this passes automatically on death.
- If the administration is disputed or if a person intends to make a claim as a dependant or member of the family, his or her claim is 'statute-barred' six months after the grant of probate. The right to take action remains open if the estate is administered without probate. This does not matter much with small estates but would be very risky for the administrator of a more substantial estate.
- A lay executor who managed to call in the assets of an estate without probate might miss the obligation to report matters to the Inland Revenue for inheritance tax purposes, especially where a substantial gift had been made in the seven years prior to the death.

When and why letters of administration are needed

If someone dies intestate – that is, without making a will – the rules of intestacy laid down by Act of Parliament apply. As administrator, you have to apply for letters of administration for exactly the same reasons as the executor has to apply for probate. You may run into difficulties if someone else in the family is equally entitled to apply for letters of administration and you cannot agree who should apply. Generally speaking, the grant is made to the first applicant but, in the event of a dispute between equally entitled administrators, the Registrar of the Probate Registry should be consulted.

'Letters of administration with will annexed'

If a will deals with part but not all of the administration (for instance where the will says who gets what but fails to appoint an executor), the person entitled to apply for letters of administration makes the application to the registrar attaching the will at the same time. The applicant, called the administrator in this case, is granted 'Letters of administration with will annexed'. The applicant can now distribute the estate in accordance with the will or, if the will fails to cover an essential point, in accordance with the rules of intestacy.

Who can apply for letters of administration?

The following list shows the order of those entitled to apply:

- the surviving spouse (but not an unmarried partner)
- the children or their descendants (once over 18): hence, if the children of the deceased person have already died but there is a grandchild who has reached 18, that grandchild can apply for letters of administration for his or her grand-parent
- if there are no children or descendants of those children who are able to apply, the parent of the deceased can apply
- brothers and sisters 'of the whole blood' (for explanation, see page 106)
- brothers and sisters 'of the half blood'
- grandparents
- aunts and uncles of the whole blood
- aunts and uncles of the half blood
- the Crown (or Duchy of Lancaster or Duchy of Cornwall) if there are no blood relations.

Where the estate is insolvent, other creditors have the right to apply

Attending the probate registry

Your first step is to obtain the necessary forms from the personal application department of the Principal Probate Registry in London or your local district probate registry.

Straightforward cases can be handled mainly by post with only one visit to a probate registry. First, the executor completes and sends in the forms, so that they can be checked and the amounts of probate fees and inheritance tax assessed. The registry officials prepare the official document which the executor then has to swear to be true, attending personally at the registry to do so. The whole process from submission of the form to swearing the papers normally takes about five weeks. If further enquiries have to be made, it can take considerably longer.

The time can also vary considerably between the different probate registries. Some of the small local probate offices are manned only once a fortnight or even once a month. If you want, you can find out from the registries in advance which is likely to be the quickest. But bear in mind that you must visit the registry in person at least once, and possibly more often, so choose one which is convenient.

Filling in probate forms

Read this section when you have the forms in front of you. These come from the probate registry for you to complete:

- form PA1 – the probate application form
- form IHT 205 – the return of assets and debts.

Also in the package are four other items as guidance:

- IHT 206 – notes to help you fill in IHT 205
- form PA1(A) – guidance notes for completing PA1
- form PA3 – a list of local probate offices
- form PA4 – a table of fees payable.

Form PA1

This is quite simple to complete. As the blue parts are for official use, only the white sections need to be completed. First the form asks which office the applicant wants to attend, next for details about the deceased, the will and about you (see the sample form on pages 62–65). In cases where more than one executor is involved, the registry normally corresponds directly with one executor only

The form has a space for naming any executors who cannot apply for probate, for example because they do not want to act or have died since the will was written. If they might apply later, the probate office sends an official 'power reserved' letter which the non-acting executor signs. This is a useful safeguard in case the first executor dies or becomes incapacitated before the grant of probate is obtained.

You do not have to sign form PA1. At the end of the process, the probate registry turns the information you supply into the stipulated legal language for the document you are required to sign.

Form PA1 contains a reminder that you have to attach the death certificate, the will and the completed form IHT 205. If this reveals that the estate exceeds the 'excepted estate' threshold (that is, the size of the estate where inheritance tax becomes due), form IHT 200 will have to be completed. *Note*: Do not attach the will to anything by clip or a staple as it will cause problems at the probate registry.

Click here to clear your text

Probate Application Form - PA1

Please use BLOCK CAPITALS

SAMPLE

Name of deceased	Surname
	Forenames

Please state where you wish to be interviewed (see enclosed address list) and specify dates you will not be available for interview

Please read the following questions and PA2 booklet 'How to obtain probate' carefully before filling in this form. Please also refer to the Guidance Notes enclosed where an item is marked *.

Section A: The Will / Codicil

This column is for official use

*A1 Did the deceased leave a will/codicil? (Note: These may not necessarily be formal documents. If the answer to question 1 is Yes, you must enclose the **original** document(s) with your application.)

Yes ☐   No ☐

If No please go to Section B

Date of will/codicil

A2 Is there anyone under 18 years old who receives anything in the will/codicil?

Yes ☐   No ☐

A3 Are there any executors named in the will/codicil?

Yes ☐   No ☐

*A4 Give the names of those executors who are not applying and the reasons why. Please see attached Guidance Notes.

Names	Reason A,B,C,D,E

*B1 - B6 Please refer to the Guidance Notes.

Please state the **number** of relatives in each category (i.e. B1, B2 etc.). If there are no relatives in a particular category, write 'nil' and move onto the next category.

Once you have indicated that there are relatives in a particular category, you should go straight to Section B7. You do not need to complete the rest of this part of Section B.

Section B: Relatives of the deceased

Number (if none, write nil)	Under 18	Over 18
B1 Lawful husband or wife		
B2a Sons or daughters who survived the deceased		
b Sons or daughters who did not survive the deceased		
c Children of person(s) indicated at '2b' who survived the deceased		
B3 Parents who survived the deceased		
B4a Brothers or sisters who survived the deceased		
b Brothers or sisters who did not survive the deceased		
c Children of person(s) indicated at '4b' who survived the deceased		
B5 Grandparents who survived the deceased		
B6a Uncles or aunts who survived the deceased		
b Uncles or aunts who did not survive the deceased		
c Children of person(s) indicated at '6b' who survived the deceased		

PA1 - Probate Application Form (4.01)

Printed on behalf of The Court Service

*B7 Was the deceased adopted?

Yes ☐   No ☐

*B8 Has any relative of the deceased been adopted?

Yes ☐   No ☐

(If Yes, give name and relationship to deceased.)

Relationship:

B9 Answer this section only if the deceased died before 4th April 1988 or left a will or codicil dated before that date.

Was the deceased illegitimate?

Yes ☐   No ☐

Did the deceased leave any illegitimate sons or daughters?

Yes ☐   No ☐

Did the deceased have any illegitimate sons or daughters who died leaving children of their own?

Yes ☐   No ☐

Section C: Details of applicant(s)

Please note that the grant will normally be sent to the first applicant. Any applicant named will be required to attend an interview. It is, however, usually only necessary for one person to apply (please see PA2 booklet, page 3).

C1   Title

Mr ☐ Mrs ☐ Miss ☐ Ms ☐ Other ☐

C2   Forenames

C3   Surname

C4   Address

Postcode:

C5   Telephone number

Home
Work

C6 Are you related to the deceased?

Yes ☐   No ☐

If Yes what is your relationship?

Relationship:

C7 Name and address of any surviving husband or wife of the deceased, unless stated above.

Postcode:

*C8 If you are applying as an attorney on behalf of the person entitled to the grant, please state their name, address and capacity in which they are entitled (e.g. relationship to the deceased).

Postcode:

Relationship:

This column is for official use

I.T.W.C

63

C9 If there are any other applicants, give their details; up to a maximum of three. (Note: All applicants named on this form must attend an interview.)

Details of other applicants who wish to be named in the grant of representation. (Please give details as C1 to C6.)

This column is for official use

Section D: Details of the deceased

*D1 Forenames

*D2 Surname

True name

*D3 Did the deceased hold any assets (excluding joint assets) in another name?

Yes [ ]   No [ ]

Alias

*D4 If Yes, what are the assets?

And in what name(s) are they held?

D5 Last permanent address of the deceased.

Address

Postcode:

D6 Date of birth

D7 Date of death

Age:

D/C district and No.

D8 Was England and Wales the permanent home of the deceased? If No, please specify the deceased's permanent home.

Yes [ ]   No [ ]

L.S.A.

D.B.F.

*D9 Tick the last legal marital status of the deceased, and give dates where appropriate.

Bachelor/Spinster [ ]

Widowed [ ]

Married [ ]   Date:

Divorced [ ]   Date:

Note: These documents (+) may usually be obtained from the Court which processed the divorce/separation.

(If the deceased did not leave a will, please enclose official copy* of the Decree Absolute.)

Judicially separated [ ]   Date:

(If the deceased did not leave a will, please enclose official copy* of the Decree of Judicial Separation.)

Important - please complete the checklist overleaf before submitting your application

Important

Checklist

Before sending your application, please complete this checklist to confirm that you have enclosed the following items:

1 PA1 (Probate Application Form) ☐

2 IHT205 / D18 (signed) ☐

3 Original will and codicil(s) ☐

4 Official copy of death certificate or coroner's letter ☐

5 Please state total amount of cheque enclosed for fee (made payable to HMPG) including cost for the number of official copy grants required at £1 each.
Please state at 6 below, how many copies you require.

£ _____

6 Number of official copy grants required (please state if sealed and certified copies are required – see PA3)

_____

7 Other documents as requested on PA1 – please specify

_____

Note: If you do not enclose all the relevant items, your application may be delayed.

Official Use Only

Type of grant:

Power reserved to _____ [Name of executor/s]

Will message: with a codicil / and _____ codicils (delete as appropriate)

Limitation _____

Min interest   Yes / No

Life interest   Yes / No

Figures:- DNE / amounts to Gross: £
                            Net: £   Fee Paid: £ _____

Clearing:-

Title:-

Footnote:-

Form IHT 205

You do not have to sign form PA1. At the end of the process, the probate registry turns the information you supply into the stipulated legal language for the document you are required to sign.

Form PA1 contains a reminder of the documents you must send in including form IHT 205 (see sample form, opposite). If this reveals that the value of the estate exceeds the 'excepted threshold' (i.e., the value of the estate where inheritance tax becomes payable), form IHT 200 will have to be completed.

Form IHT 205 is used by the probate registry to weed out those estates which are below the tax threshold (the nil band rate). If the gross estate is less than £210,000 (rates for 2000–1), there is no need to fill in the more detailed form IHT 200 unless the Inland Revenue Capital Taxes Office asks you to do so. If the estate is more than £210,000, you will have to complete form IHT 200. If that is the case, see 'Inheritance tax and form IHT 200', later in this chapter.

Inland Revenue
Capital Taxes

Short Form for Personal Applicants

SAMPLE

Name of the person who has died	Date when the person died*

*Use this form only if the person died after 6 April 2000

Inheritance Tax

Introduction

Do you need to fill in a full Inland Revenue Account before you can get a grant of probate?

Probate fees and any Inheritance Tax and interest due have to be worked out and paid before you can get a grant of probate or letters of administration.

Estates which meet certain conditions are called "excepted estates". If the estate of the person who has died is an excepted estate, you do not need to fill in a full Inheritance Tax Account. You can fill in this form instead.

Before you start to fill in this form, read the introduction in the booklet IHT 206. This will help you to decide whether you should fill in this form or a full Inheritance Tax Account on form IHT 200.

Question 1
Where was the domicile of the person who has died? (Please tick one box only.)

England and Wales ☐   Scotland ☐

Northern Ireland ☐   Other ☐

If you ticked "other", do not fill in any more of this form. Instead you will need to fill in a full Inland Revenue Account on form IHT200. You can get one by telephoning IR Capital Taxes on 0845 2341020. This is an answer phone service.

If you did not tick "other" please answer the questions on page 2. If you answer 'No' to all of them, look at the booklet IHT 206 again to help you to fill in pages 3 and 4. **If you find that you need more space, use a separate sheet of paper and show clearly which part of the form the sheet refers to.** When you have filled in the whole form and signed it, send it to the Probate Registry with form PA1.

Do you need help?

If you have any questions about **Inheritance Tax** or how to fill in this form, please write to:-

Inland Revenue Capital Taxes, Ferrers House, PO Box 38, Castle Meadow Road, Nottingham, NG2 1BB

or telephone 0115 974 2400 (please do not use this number just to order form IHT200).

If you have any questions about **Probate** matters, please contact your local District Probate Registry.

IHT205   *1*   095331012001DTP

Questions			*please tick*	
2. Gifts			**Yes**	**No**

Did the person who has died within 7 years of the date they died,

		Yes	No
a	make any gifts or set up a trust? (but see note on page 2 of IHT206)	☐	☐
b	make any payment(s) of more than £10,000 in total for the maintenance of a relative?	☐	☐
c	pay any premiums on a life insurance policy under which the benefit is not payable to the personal representative or to the husband or wife of the person who has died?	☐	☐
3.	Did the person who has died make a **gift with reservation** at any time?	☐	☐

4. Assets held in trust

Was the person who has died receiving a benefit under a trust

	Yes	No
• at the time when they died	☐	☐
• at any time within 7 years before they died?	☐	☐

5. Foreign assets

	Yes	No
Did the person who has died own or benefit from any assets outside the United Kingdom whose value is more than £50,000?	☐	☐

If you have answered 'Yes' to any of these questions, do not fill in pages 3 and 4 of this form. Instead you will need to fill in a full Inland Revenue Account on form IHT200.

You can get one from IR Capital Taxes by telephoning our Orderline on 0845 2341020. This is an answer phone service. We will aim to send forms out to you by the end of the next working day.

2

3. Return of the whole estate

Assets in the United Kingdom except for joint assets passing
automatically to the surviving joint owner.

Value in £s

1. Cash other than at bank ....

2. Money in bank accounts ....

3. Money in building societies, co-operative or friendly societies or
   savings banks including interest to the date of death ....

4. Household and personal goods, *for example, furniture, jewellery, car,
   stamp collections etc* ....

5. Savings Certificates and other National Savings investments ....

6. Stocks and shares quoted on the Stock Exchange ....

7. Stocks and shares not quoted on the Stock Exchange ....

8. Insurance policies including bonuses on 'with profits' policies and
   mortgage protection policies ....

9. Amounts which employers owe - including arrears of salary and
   pension payable to the estate ....

10. Partnership and business interests ....

11. Freehold and leasehold property **in the sole name of the person who
    has died.** (Address(es)) ....

12. Assets held as tenants in common ....

13. Any other assets not included above, for example, income tax
    repayment, debt or other amount owing to the person who has died ....

Total £ | A

14. Assets outside the United Kingdom (Value in sterling) ....

15. Nominated assets ....

16. **Joint assets passing automatically to the surviving joint owner**

Details of joint assets ....

Value of whole of joint assets £ ....

Share of person who has died (eg half) .... Value of that share

Total gross estate (A + 14 + 15 + 16) = £ | B

17. **Gifts of cash, or stocks and shares quoted on the Stock Exchange** ....

Total for excepted estate (B + 17) = £ | C*

* see the box on the back page of this form   *3*

69

18. Debts

Bills owing in the United Kingdom

Funeral expenses .... £ [   ]

Debts owed by the person who has died .... £ [   ]

Mortgage on a property in the name
of the person who has died .... £ [   ]

Total debts owing in the UK £ [   ] D

Debts owing to persons outside the UK .... £ [   ] P

Debts secured on or payable out of joint assets ... £ [   ] Q

Total debts (D+P+Q) = £ [   ] E

Net figure for Inheritance Tax (C minus E) .... £ [   ] F

Signature(s) [   ]

Date

* **If the figure at C is less than £210,000,** you do not have to fill in an Account on form IHT 200. **However, IR Capital Taxes has the right to call for an Account within 35 days of the grant. It calls for an Account in a small number of cases each year.** The Probate Registry will return this form to you when they issue the grant of probate. Please keep this form safe so that if you do receive a request for an Account from Capital Taxes, you can send them a copy.

Unless they make such a request within 35 days of the date of the grant, you have automatic clearance from Inheritance Tax as long as you have made a full disclosure of all relevant facts.

Summary

Gross estate in United Kingdom passing under Will/intestacy £ [   ] A

Debts in United Kingdom owed by deceased alone £ [   ] D

Net estate in United Kingdom (A-D) £ [   ] G

4

Sending off the forms

If the estate you are administering can be contained on form IHT 205, you will be in a position to submit your application. Take a copy of all the material. The registry supplies a large envelope with the forms. You should send the following:

- the will (not clipped or stapled to any other paper)
- the death certificate
- probate application form PA1
- short form IHT 205
- a cheque for the fee and for copies.

Attach any explanatory letter or schedule as necessary. Then send the package by registered post to the probate registry. A few weeks later, you are invited to review the documents, pay the probate fee and swear the prescribed oath. For this interview – see below – remember to take your file of background papers.

Fees

Probate fees are charges made by the probate registry for dealing with the papers and issuing the grant of probate. They are calculated on the amount of the net estate, as declared for the purpose of inheritance tax (excluding any part of the estate passing by survivorship). Fees are payable when you attend the interview at the registry – see form PA4 for guidance.

At the probate registry

When you reach the registry on the agreed day, the information you supplied on the probate forms has been transferred in formal legal language to printed documents. The executor's oath and Inland Revenue account have also been prepared. Details of the life, death and family of, for example, Mary Josephine Blake and her property have been included too. As executor, you have to satisfy yourself that the details in the forms are true in every respect. When you have done this, the commissioner asks you to sign the original will and swear the oath, identifying the will as that of Mary Blake.

You stand up, hold a copy of the New Testament and, repeating the words spoken by the commissioner, say: 'I swear by Almighty God that this is my name and handwriting and that the contents of this my oath are true and that this is the will referred to'. The form of the oath is varied for people of non-Christian religions or those who have other grounds for objecting to swearing on the New Testament.

The commissioner signs beneath your signatures on the official form and the will. You now pay the probate fees. It is best, too, to order a number of 'sealed' copies of the grant of probate when it is completed. These enable you to call in the estate's assets from a range of sources at the same time.

Letters of administration

If Mrs Blake, for example, has left no will, her next of kin – her children or one of them – applies for a grant of letters of administration instead of probate. The same is the case if she left a will but did not appoint executors. In those cases, the grant is called 'letters of administration with will annexed'.

When letters of administration are being sought, the administrators may in some cases have to provide a guarantee – for example, where the beneficiaries are under age or mentally disabled or when the administrator is out of the country. The guarantee is provided by an insurance company at a cost or by individuals who undertake to make good – up to the gross value of the estate – any deficiency caused by the administrators failing in their duties.

Letters of administration may also be taken out by creditors of an estate if executors deliberately do not apply for probate – for instance, if the estate has insufficient assets to pay all the creditors and legatees.

Inheritance tax and form IHT 200

Form IHT 200 is the Inland Revenue account for inheritance tax (see the sample form on pages 76–83). It should be completed by reference to form IHT 210, which contains guidance notes to help you and includes a completed specimen form IHT 200.

IHT 200 consists of eight pages. The first page requires the name of the Registry to which you are applying (section A) followed by details of the deceased, their surviving relatives and other information such as their National Insurance number and income tax district (section B). It also asks for details of the person dealing with the estate (section C).

Page 2 asks 18 questions to which the answers will be yes or no. These range from 'Did the deceased leave a will?' to 'Did the deceased own any stocks or shares?' and 'Did the deceased own any assets outside the UK?'

If your answer to any of the questions is yes you will have to fill in a numbered supplementary page which will have to be ordered from the Capital Taxes Office orderline. The supplementary pages are also colour coded.

In Mrs Blake's case the supplementary pages will be needed in respect of the following questions:

- Did the deceased leave a will?: yes – Page D1
- Did the deceased have provisions for a pension other than the state pension?: yes – Page D6
- Did the deceased own any stocks and shares?: yes – Page 7
- Did the deceased own any household goods or other personal possessions?: yes – page D10
- Did the deceased own any land or buildings in the UK?: yes – Page D12
- National Savings, bank and building society investments and other personal assets must be entered on supplementary sheet D17.

Having completed page 2 and the supplementary pages you can look at page 3. Section E asks about domicile in Scotland but Section F on page 3 is headed 'Estate in the UK where tax may not be paid by instalments'. Estate where inheritance tax may be paid by instalments consists of land and houses, buildings, business property, farm woodland and certain other assets. If an asset does not fall into that instalment category it must be included in the column of boxes which are set out on page 3. These boxes will contain the totals set out in the supplementary pages referred to.

For example, the first and second boxes on page 3 show the total value of quoted stocks, shares and investments (box F1) and UK government and municipal securities (box F2) taken from supplementary page D7.

Page 4 itemises liabilities, funeral expenses and exemptions and reliefs which, after being deducted from the total value of the estate in the UK on page 3, gives the chargeable value of assets in the UK where tax may not be paid by instalments.

Page 5 (section G) provides boxes for showing the value of the estate where tax may be paid by instalments. These boxes refer to the house of the deceased, farms, business property and other eligible property. The boxes also provide for the deduction of mortgages exemptions and relief from those figures. The final box on page 5 gives the chargeable value of assets in the UK where tax may be paid by instalments.

Page 6 (section H) provides a column of boxes into which the value of other taxable items must be brought in order to work out the total value of the property liable to tax on the death of the deceased. It is on this page that the value of other items such as jointly owned property, foreign property and settled (trust) property are brought into the calculations. It is also on this page that the value of lifetime gifts, which are not exempt, must be brought into the calculations.

Page 7 (section J) provides a layout of boxes for calculating the tax liability. If you do not wish to do the calculation yourself, you may leave sections H and J blank in which case the

Capital Taxes Office will complete the calculations from the figures you have provided.

Page 8 (section L) contains a declaration which you should read as it places an obligation on the executor or administrator to make the fullest enquiries they can to discover the assets of the estate and to report their open market value.

The final step before probate is granted is for the executor to pay inheritance tax on the estate's assets as assessed by the Capital Taxes Office of the Inland Revenue. This has to be paid before the assets of the estate are available to cover it. Banks are well used to this situation and there should be no problem arranging a short-term loan to pay the tax. *Note* that interest, at a variable rate, is charged on all outstanding inheritance tax from the end of the sixth month after death.

Where the assets consist of land and farmland, a family business and some unquoted shares, you can pay inheritance tax by instalments in ten yearly payments. (The whole of the outstanding tax becomes due immediately if the property is sold). In the case of farmland and business assets alone, interest runs from the date an instalment is due. *Note* that where it is allowed, the instalments option is worth considering. It delays payment of most of the tax until after the grant of probate and you therefore reduce the interest you have to pay on a loan or overdraft. Loan interest is generally higher than that charged on overdue tax.

Inland Revenue Account for Inheritance Tax

Inland Revenue
Capital Taxes

Fill in this account for the estate of a person who died on or after 18 March 198_.
You should read the related guidance note(s) before filling in any particular box(_).
The notes follow the same numbering as this form, so section headings are shown
by capital letters and the items in each section are on a dark background.

A **Probate Registry, Commissary Court or Sheriff Court District**

Name A1   Date of Grant

B **About the person who has died**

Title B1   Surname B2

First name(s) B3

Date of birth B4 / /   Date of death B5 / /

Marital status B6   Last known usual address

Surviving relatives   B7

Husband/Wife B8

Brother(s)/Sister(s) B9

Parent(s) B10   Postcode

Number of   Nursing / Residential home B13

Children B11   Domicile B14

Grandchildren B12   Occupation B15

National Insurance number B16

Income tax district B17

Income tax reference or self assessment reference B18

C **Solicitor or other person to contact**

Name and address of firm or person
dealing with the estate

C1   Telephone number

C4

Fax number

C5

Postcode

For IR CT use

DX number and town

C2 DX

Contact name and reference

C3

IHT 200

Ⓓ Supplementary pages

You must answer all of the questions in this section. You should read the notes starting at page 10 of form IHT 210 before answering the questions.

If you answer "Yes" to a question you will need to fill in the supplementary page shown. If you do not have all the supplementary pages you need you should telephone our Orderline on 0845 2341000

		No	Yes	Page
● The Will	Did the deceased leave a Will?	☐	☐	➡ D1
● Domicile outside the United Kingdom	Was the deceased domiciled outside the UK at the date of death?	☐	☐	➡ D2
● Gifts and other transfers of value	Did the deceased make any gift or any other transfer of value on or after 18 March 1986?	☐	☐	➡ D3
● Joint assets	Did the deceased hold any asset(s) in joint names with another person?	☐	☐	➡ D4
● Nominated assets	Did the deceased, at any time during their lifetime, give written instructions (usually called a "nomination") that any asset was to pass to a particular person on their death?	☐	☐	➡ D4
● Assets held in trust	Did the deceased have any right to any benefit from any assets held in trust or in a settlement at the date of death?	☐	☐	D5
● Pensions	Did the deceased have provision for a pension from employers, a personal pension policy or other provisions made for retirement other than the State Pension?	☐	☐	➡ D6
● Stocks and shares	Did the deceased own any stocks or shares?	☐	☐	D7
● Debts due to the estate	Did the deceased lend any money, either on mortgage or by personal loan, that had not been repaid by the date of death?	☐	☐	➡ D8
● Life insurance and annuities	Did the deceased pay any premiums on any life insurance policies or annuities which are payable to either the estate or to someone else or which continue after death?	☐	☐	➡ D9
● Household and personal goods	Did the deceased own any household goods or other personal possessions?	☐	☐	➡ D10
● Interest in another estate	Did the deceased have a right to a legacy or a share of an estate of someone who died before them, but which they had not received before they died?	☐	☐	D11
● Land, buildings and interests in land	Did the deceased own any land or buildings in the UK?	☐	☐	D12
● Agricultural relief	Are you deducting agricultural relief?	☐	☐	➡ D13
● Business interests	Did the deceased own all or part of a business or were they a partner in a business?	☐	☐	➡ D14
● Business relief	Are you deducting business relief?	☐	☐	➡ D14
● Foreign assets	Did the deceased own any assets outside the UK?	☐	☐	D15
● Debts owed by the estate	Are you claiming a deduction against the estate for any money that the deceased had borrowed from relatives, close friends, or trustees, or other loans, overdrafts or guarantee debts?	☐	☐	➡ D16

E **Domicile in Scotland**

- Has any claim for legal rights been made or discharged?   No ☐ Yes ☐
- How many children are under 18 ☐ or 18 and over ☐

F **Estate in the UK where tax may not be paid by instalments**

- Quoted stocks, shares and investments *(box SS1, form D7)* — **F1** £ _____
- UK Government and municipal securities *(box SS2, form D7)* — **F2** £ _____
- Unquoted stocks, shares and investments — **F3** £ _____
- Traded unquoted stocks and shares — **F4** £ _____
- Dividends or interest — **F5** £ _____
- Premium Bonds — **F6** £ _____
- National Savings investments *(show details on form D17)* — **F7** £ _____
- Bank and building society accounts *(show details on form D17)* — **F8** £ _____
- Cash — **F9** £ _____
- Debts due to the deceased and secured by mortgage *(box DD1, form D8)* — **F10** £ _____
- Other debts due to the deceased *(box DD1, form D8)* — **F11** £ _____
- Rents due to the deceased — **F12** £ _____
- Accrued income — **F13** £ _____
- Apportioned income — **F14** £ _____
- Other income due to the deceased *(box IP4, form D9, box PA1 form D6)* — **F15** £ _____
- Life insurance policies *(box IP3, form D9)* — **F16** £ _____
- Private health schemes — **F17** £ _____
- Income tax or capital gains tax repayment — **F18** £ _____
- Household and personal goods *(sold, box HG1, form D10)* — **F19** £ _____
- Household and personal goods *(unsold, box HG2, form D10)* — **F20** £ _____
- Interest in another estate *(box UE1, form D11)* — **F21** £ _____
- Interest in expectancy (reversionary interest) — **F22** £ _____
- Other personal assets in the UK *(show details on form D17)* — **F23** £ _____

Total assets *(sum of boxes F1 to F23)* — **F24** £ _____

3

Liabilities, funeral expenses, exemptions and reliefs

- Liabilities

Name	Description of liability	

Total liabilities **F25** £

- Funeral expenses

Total of funeral expenses **F26** £

Total liabilities and funeral expenses *(box F25 plus box F26)* **F27** £

Net total of assets less liabilities *(box F24 less box F27)* **F28** £

- Exemptions and reliefs

Total exemptions and reliefs **F29** £

Chargeable value of assets in the UK where tax may not be paid by instalments *(box F28 less box F29)* **F30** £

4

Ⓖ Estate in the UK where tax may be paid by instalments

Do you wish to pay the tax on these assets by instalments? No Yes

- Deceased's residence — G1 £
- Other residential property — G2 £
- Farms — G3 £
- Business property — G4 £
- Timber and woodland — G5 £
- Other land and buildings — G6 £

	Interest in a business	Interest in a partnership	
Farming business	G7.1 £	G7.2 £	G7 £

	Interest in a business	Interest in a partnership	
Other business interests	G8.1 £	G8.2 £	G8 £

	Farm trade assets	Other business assets	
Business assets	G9.1 £	G9.2 £	G9 £

- Quoted shares and securities, control holding only — G10 £

	Control holding	Non-control holding	
Unquoted shares	G11.1 £	G11.2 £	G11 £

	Control holding	Non-control holding	
Traded unquoted shares	G12.1 £	G12.2 £	G12 £

Total assets *(sum of boxes G1 to G12)* — G13 £

Liabilities, exemptions and reliefs

- Name and address of mortgagee

G14 £

- Other liabilities

Total of other liabilities G15 £

Net total of assets less liabilities *(box G13 less boxes G14 and G15)* G16 £

- Exemptions and reliefs

Total exemptions and reliefs G17 £

Chargeable value of assets in the UK where tax may be paid by instalments *(box G16 less box G17)* G18 £

5

H **Summary of the chargeable estate**

You should fill in form IHT(WS) so that you can copy the figures to this section and to section J. If you are applying for a grant without the help of a solicitor or other agent and you do not wish to work out the tax yourself, leave this section and section J blank. Go on to section K.

Assets where tax may not be paid by instalments

- Estate in the UK *(box WS1)* H1 £
- Joint property *(box WS2)* H2 £
- Foreign property *(box WS3)* H3 £
- Settled property on which the trustees would like to pay tax now *(box WS4)* H4 £

    Total of assets where tax may not be paid by instalments *(box WS5)* H5 £

Assets where tax may be paid by instalments

- Estate in the UK *(box WS6)* H6 £
- Joint property *(box WS7)* H7 £
- Foreign property *(box WS8)* H8 £
- Settled property on which the trustees would like to pay tax now *(box WS9)* H9 £

    Total of assets where tax may be paid by instalments *(box WS10)* H10 £

Other property taken into account to calculate the total tax

- Settled property *(box WS11)* H11 £
- Gift with reservation *(box WS12)* H12 £

    Chargeable estate *(box WS13)* H13 £

    Cumulative total of lifetime transfers *(box WS14)* H14 £

    Aggregate chargeable transfer *(box WS15)* H15 £

6

81

J **Calculating the tax liability**

Calculating the total tax that is payable

- Aggregate chargeable transfer *(box WS16)* — **J1** £
- Tax threshold *(box WS17)* — **J2** £
- Value chargeable to tax *(box WS18)* — **J3** £

Tax payable *(box WS19)* **J4** £

- Tax (if any) payable on lifetime transfers *(box WS20)* — **J5** £
- Relief for successive charges *(box WS21)* — **J6** £

Tax payable on total of assets liable to tax *(box WS22)* **J7** £

Calculating the tax payable on delivery of this account

- Tax which may not be paid by instalments *(box TX4)* — **J8** £
- Double taxation relief *(box TX5)* — **J9** £
- Interest to be added *(box TX7)* — **J10** £

Tax and interest being paid now which may
not be paid by instalments *(box TX8)* **J11** £

- Tax which may be paid by instalments *(box TX12)* — **J12** £
- Double taxation relief *(box TX13)* — **J13** £
- Number of instalments being paid now **J14** / 10 *(box TX15)*
- Tax now payable *(box TX16)* — **J15** £
- Interest on instalments to be added *(box TX17)* — **J16** £
- Additional interest to be added *(box TX18)* — **J17** £

Tax and interest being paid now which may be paid by instalments *(box TX19)* **J18** £

Total tax and interest being paid now on this account *(box TX20)* **J19** £

K **Authority for repayment of inheritance tax**

In the event of any inheritance tax being overpaid the payable order for overpaid tax and interest in
connection with this estate should be made out to

7

ⓛ Declaration

I/We wish to apply for a **L1**

To the best of my/our knowledge and belief, the information I/we have given and the statements I/we have made in this account and in supplementary pages **L2**
attached (together called "this account") are correct and complete.

I/We have made the fullest enquiries that are reasonably practicable in the circumstances to find out the open market value of all the items shown in this account. The value of items in box(es)

L3 are provisional

estimates which are based on all the information available to me/us at this time. I/We will tell IR Capital Taxes the exact value(s) as soon as I/we know it and I/we will pay any additional tax and interest that may be due.

I/We understand that I/we may be liable to prosecution if I/we deliberately conceal any information that affects the liability to inheritance tax arising on the deceased's death, OR if I/we deliberately include information in this account which I/we know to be false.

I/We understand that I/we may have to pay financial penalties if this account is incorrect by reason of my/our fraud or negligence, OR if I/we fail to remedy anything in this account which is incorrect in any material respect within a reasonable time of it coming to my/our notice.

I/We understand that the issue of the grant does not mean that

- I/we have paid all the inheritance tax and interest that may be due on the estate, or
- the statements made and the values included in this account are accepted by IR Capital Taxes.

I/We understand that IR Capital Taxes

- will only look at this account in detail after the grant has been issued
- may need to ask further questions and discuss the value of items shown in this account
- may make further calculations of tax and interest payable to help the persons liable for the tax make provision to meet the tax liability.

I/We understand that where we have elected to pay tax by instalments that I/we may have to pay interest on any unpaid tax according to the law.

Each person delivering this account, whether as executor, intending administrator or otherwise must sign below to indicate that they have read and agreed the statements above.

Full name and address	Full name and address
Signature　　　Date	Signature　　　Date
Full name and address	Full name and address
Signature　　　Date	Signature　　　Date

The grant of probate

There may be an interval of six weeks or more between lodging the probate papers and the meeting at the registry to sign and swear them. After that, things move quickly. If there is no inheritance tax to be paid – where the net estate is less than £242,000 or where all the deceased's property goes to the spouse – the grant of probate (or letters of administration) is issued within a few days. If inheritance tax is due, it takes two or three weeks before the exact amount is calculated and the grant is usually ready around a week later.

The grant of probate is signed by an officer of the Probate Registry. The essence of it reads as follows: '....the last Will and Testament (a copy of which is annexed) of the said deceased was proved and registered in the Principal Probate Registry of the High Court of Justice and administration of all the estate which by law devolves to and vests in the personal representative of the said deceased ...... granted to ......'. The document also states the gross and net estates (that is, before and after deduction of debts).

Attached to the grant of probate is a photocopy of the will. (All original wills are kept at the Principal Probate Registry in London). Each page of your copy carries the impress of the court's official seal. It is accompanied by a note which explains the procedure for collecting and distributing the estate and advises representatives to take legal advice in the event of a dispute or difficulty.

Chapter 6

Distributing the estate

Now that you have probate or letters of administration, you begin to carry out the final stages of your executorship. In both cases, the process for realising the assets and paying debts and liabilities is broadly the same. Differences arise when distribution follows either the wishes of the deceased according to a valid will or the rules of intestacy.

Calling in assets

The first step is to begin to apply to the holders of the assets of the estate for their repayment.

Banks and building societies

Complete the application forms and send them together with the passbook and office copy of the grant to the head or district office. In order to complete the tax return, ask for a final statement of interest at the same time.

National Savings

Complete the application forms and send them to the appropriate office with the certificates, passbook or Premium Bonds together with an office copy of the grant.

Stocks and shares

You may wish to transfer these into the name of a beneficiary, in which case you can obtain the forms from the Company Registrars. Otherwise you may find it easier to sell the shares through your bank or through an independent stockbroker. They need office copies of the probate and share certificates (unless these are held electronically). In the case of some unit trusts, the certificates already have a sale form on the back which can be completed and submitted to the trust's administrators.

Houses

If the deceased's house has passed automatically to the co-owner, you can now hand over the deeds. If it is wholly owned by the deceased, it may have been left to a particular person by a gift set out in the will or sold to raise money to distribute to beneficiaries.

If the house or flat is to be sold, the executor usually instructs an estate agent to find a buyer and a solicitor to carry out the actual transfer. The executor could find a buyer him- or herself but, if any beneficiary believes that he or she has not got a proper price, he or she could sue the executor for negligence. For this reason, unless you have the relevant professional qualifications, it is not advisable to sell or transfer a property yourself without a professional valuation.

Paying the debts

As cheques arrive from banks and building societies, and from the sale of investments and the house, you can begin to pay outstanding debts.

Income tax

By this stage you should have received a tax return for the period covering 6 April to the date of death. It is your responsibility to complete it. In most cases the tax return is straightforward, except where the deceased has recently sold shares or other assets. This may give rise to a charge to capital gains tax, which must be paid before the distribution begins.

Household debts

Final readings for water, gas, electricity and telephone may need to be organised. Once the house is empty, you should ask the local authority to provide a final Council Tax account. Check with the council whether charges are waived while you try to sell the house.

If you have employed an accountant to prepare the tax return, you have his or her account to settle, together with other accounts for, say, essential house or car repairs. Once you have made reasonable enquiries and the time limit set out in the notice to the *London Gazette* (see page 171) has run out, you can begin to prepare for the final distribution of the estate.

Distribution of the estate according to the will

Before you distribute the estate, it is your legal duty to understand exactly what the will says. Some phrases may be difficult to interpret; others may seem clear but have a special legal meaning. Remember that an executor can be sued for payment by an aggrieved beneficiary who thinks you have interpreted the will wrongly. See Chapter 10.

Specific legacies and bequests

Legacies are usually payments of specific sums. Bequests usually mean gifts of goods or cash as opposed to 'devises', which mean gifts of land or buildings. If the estate is not subject to inheritance tax and the legacies and bequests are small in relation to the estate's assets, legacies can now be paid and specific items handed over. It is usual to request a receipt from the beneficiaries when they receive their gift or legacy. Problems can arise if it is not possible to find a beneficiary or he or she is under 18. It may also be clear that the estate is not large enough to cover the payment of the legacies in full.

Specific bequests such as jewellery, paintings and furniture, are straightforward. Always remember to maintain insurance cover until they are distributed. Give beneficiaries all documents regarding them.

Transferring a house or other property

If the will specifies a house or other property as a bequest to a beneficiary, the executor must first deal with any outstanding mortgage. The will may direct the executor to pay off the mortgage before it is transferred or that the property is to be given subject to the existing mortgage. If the will says nothing on this point, the mortgage becomes the responsibility of the beneficiary.

Registered property

You next have to deal with the transfer of the property. In most cases, property is registered at HM Land Registry. If the mortgage is to be repaid by the estate, ask the mortgage lender concerned for a redemption figure which you pay off from the executor's account. At the same time, request the charge certificate and the Land Registry form DN1 confirming repayment. Do not forget to check the insurance cover on the property. If it has been previously arranged through the building society, it may lapse automatically and need to be renewed with a separate policy.

If you decide to deal with the transfer yourself, first obtain Land Registry form AS1 from law stationers. When completed, this can be sent with the charge certificate, the completed form DN1 and the appropriate fee to the Land Registry in whose district the property is situated. The Land Registry amends the register to remove any reference to the mortgage and to show the new owner. Any continuing obligations such as covenants must be included in the AS1 form. This is signed by the beneficiary who takes over responsibility for them. Once the registration is completed, you receive the new deed – a land certificate, rather than charge certificate, as it will by then be free from any mortgage – and send it to the new owner.

Unregistered property

The process of transferring unregistered property is more complicated. You first pay off the mortgage and prepare the AS1 form. Then you apply to the Land Registry for first registration. If the Land Registry finds an irregularity with the deeds (for instance, if the deed plan does not match up with the actual boundary), you will receive some 'requisitions'.

These are detailed comments on the registration and can raise complicated issues. Seek legal advice.

Preparing the final accounts

By the time you have gathered in the assets and have started paying the debts, you have a reasonable idea of the total value of the estate. You can now begin to prepare the final accounts. There is no set form but the accounts must include assets and liabilities (the capital account), receipts and payments made during the administration (the income account) and a distribution account of payments to beneficiaries. An introductory memorandum to the accounts is often helpful to beneficiaries and should cover the following:

- details of the deceased, date of death, date of probate and names of the executors
- a summary of the bequests made in the will (or an outline of the relevant intestacy provisions)
- particulars of any property transfers
- particulars of any unusually complicated aspect of the administration
- reference to any schedules or valuations which have been included with the accounts.

In estates where inheritance tax has been paid, prepare one part of the capital account based on the value of the assets at the date of death. (These are identical to the figures in form IHT 200 – see pages 76–83).

The second part of the account should show the value of those assets and liabilities at the date they are realised or paid. If the net effect is to reduce the value of the estate, you may be able to claim a refund from the Capital Taxes Office. Conversely, you could have increased tax to pay. In either case you must advise the Capital Taxes Office of any subsequent addition to or deletion from the figures on which the change to inheritance tax has been based.

Capital, income and distribution accounts

A typical set of accounts is set out on pages 95–8. The capital account shows the value of the assets when they are cashed or realised and the debts are the sums actually paid. If you make sure that all sums are paid into your executor's bank account and that all debts are paid from it, there should be no difficulty balancing the accounts. The balance shown is the amount available for distribution, subject only to you making sure that your executor cheques, including those for specific legacies, have all been cashed. This final amount is included in the distribution account.

The income account shows the income received during the administration, less associated expenses. It is convenient to run this account from the date of death to the following 5 April. The same figures can then go in your tax return of the administration. If the administration period overruns April in any year, a second income account is prepared.

The distribution account shows the capital and income transferred from the respective accounts and how the residue of the estate has been divided. If there is only one beneficiary, you just show the final figure. If any items have been taken in kind – such as a car or a piece of furniture – its value is included in the distribution account both as an asset and payment. If you are claiming executor's expenses – travelling costs to the probate registry for example, telephone and postage – itemise them and include the total in the distribution account.

When there is a will

You have completed your accounts and paid all outstanding debts and liabilities. You can now calculate how much each residuary beneficiary receives according to the provisions of the will. The amount you have left in your executor's bank account should equal the sums to be paid out. If it does not, you need to find the mistake – a cheque not cashed, an inaccurate calculation – before taking the final steps.

First send your accounts to the beneficiaries to be sure they have no questions about them. In cases involving inheritance tax, you next confirm to the Capital Taxes Office that you have disclosed the whole value of the estate. You then apply for a clearance certificate. As soon as this certificate is to hand, you make the final distribution to the beneficiaries. They can be asked to sign an acknowledgement in the following form:

The estate of   deceased

I approve the accounts which I have seen and agree to accept

£   in full satisfaction of my entitlement to share in

this estate.

Please send me a crossed cheque in my favour to the address

shown below.

Signed...

Dated..

Address...

Deceased and missing beneficiaries

If a beneficiary dies before the death of the testator, the general rule is that the gift or legacy cannot be made. But there are important exceptions:

- if the will contains a 'substitution' (an alternate name to whom the gift or legacy goes)
- if the gift is made to two people as joint tenants (the survivor is the recipient)
- if section 33(2) of the Wills Act 1837 applies. This section provides that, if the share of the estate or gift is to a child or other descendant of the testator and the child dies before

the testator leaving 'issue' (children and their descendants), they take the share or gift.

If you cannot find a beneficiary, you must make reasonable enquiries. Advertise in the area the missing beneficiary was last heard of and write to relations or friends who might know. If your enquiries fail, consider taking out indemnity insurance to protect you against the claimant turning up and seeking his or her entitlement from you personally. Alternatively, you can apply to the court for an order (called 'Benjamin order') giving you permission to distribute the estate on agreed terms. The costs of the insurance and court fees are legitimate expenses you can claim from the estate.

Distribution according to the rules of intestacy

The general procedure for realising assets, paying debts and finalising the accounts is the same whether the distribution is by will or according to the rules of intestacy. The difference arises when you come to distribute the estate. Under the rules of intestacy, a fixed formula determines who gets what and in what order. The following diagram sets out the arrangements. *Note* that cohabitees and stepchildren are excluded from these arrangements, but they can, in certain circumstances, make claims against the estate.

The order of distribution for intestate estates

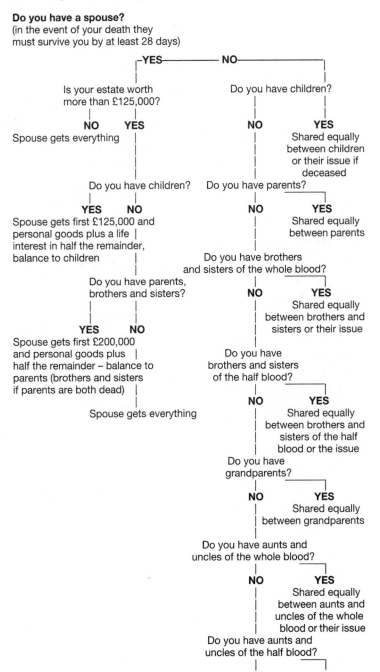

Do you have a spouse?
(in the event of your death they
must survive you by at least 28 days)

┌─YES────── NO──────────────┐

YES branch:

Is your estate worth
more than £125,000?

NO — Spouse gets everything

YES:

Do you have children?

YES — Spouse gets first £125,000 and
personal goods plus a life
interest in half the remainder,
balance to children

NO:

Do you have parents,
brothers and sisters?

YES — Spouse gets first £200,000
and personal goods plus
half the remainder – balance to
parents (brothers and sisters
if parents are both dead)

NO — Spouse gets everything

NO branch:

Do you have children?

YES — Shared equally
between children
or their issue if
deceased

NO:

Do you have parents?

YES — Shared equally
between parents

NO:

Do you have brothers
and sisters of the whole blood?

YES — Shared equally
between brothers and
sisters or their issue

NO:

Do you have
brothers and sisters
of the half blood?

YES — Shared equally
between brothers and
sisters of the half
blood or the issue

NO:

Do you have
grandparents?

YES — Shared equally
between grandparents

NO:

Do you have aunts and
uncles of the whole blood?

YES — Shared equally
between aunts and
uncles of the whole
blood or their issue

NO:

Do you have aunts and
uncles of the half blood?

```
                              NO          YES
                               |     Shared equally
                               |     between aunts and
                               |     uncles of the half
                               |     blood or their issue
                               |
                          Everything goes to
                          The Crown, the Duchy of
                        Lancaster or the Duchy of Cornwall
```

The children's trust under intestacy rules

When the surviving spouse has children, whatever their age, and the estate is worth more than £125,000, the administrators of the estate must set up a trust to look after the children's share. As trustees, they must invest half the remaining capital in their own names (after taking advice from an independent investment, or other appropriate, adviser). They notify the Inland Revenue of the new trust and submit a Trust Tax return each year. The income from the trust is paid to the spouse. On his or her death, the capital held in the trust account is shared between the children unless they are under 18. In this case, their share of the capital remains in the trust until they reach 18.

If any of the children die, leaving children of their own, before the death of their intestate or – whichever is the later – second parent, the 'Statutory Trusts' rules apply. Under these rules, where a child of the intestate has died leaving children who are 18 or over (or who marry before 18), the children (the grandchildren of the intestate) get their parent's share. The same rule applies if the only survivors are great grandchildren or even more remote descendants.

Except where a post-death variation is agreed by all the beneficiaries, intestacy rules can be troublesome and in some cases cause real hardship. For instance, where there is a house in the name of the intestate with a value in excess of £125,000, it can be difficult to give the surviving spouse £125,000 without first selling the house. The rules allow the surviving spouse to elect to take a lump sum instead of a life interest in half the remaining capital. They also permit the surviving spouse to elect to take the matrimonial home as part of their lump sum (if the lump sum is large enough to cover its value). But this still means that a spouse who is in real need of the whole of their deceased spouse's estate can only get part of it under the intestacy rules. The rules, too, make no provision for cohabitees or stepchildren.

Typical Administration Accounts

IN THE ESTATE OF MARY BLAKE DECEASED
(date of death 30 September 2001)

Capital Account
Assets

The Firs, Minford. Net sale proceeds (value at death £170,000.00).	£165,000	
Less Mortgage	£65,000	
		£100,000
Stocks and shares		£266,500
(Value at death £263,500)		
Prudential – life policy		£6,000
Halifax plc deposit	£2,500	
Plus interest to date of death	£50	
		£2,550
Yorkshire Bank plc		£600
National Savings – Premium Bonds		£200
Arrears of pension		£100
Agreed value of house contents		£2,000
Agreed value of VW Polo		£2,000
Refund of overpaid inheritance tax (on value of house)		£2,000
Gross Estate		£381,950
Less Debts and Liabilities		
Funeral account	£1,500	
Gas	£200	
Electricity	£50	
Administration expenses	£75	
Probate fees	£130	
Stockbroker's valuation fee	£250	
Income tax paid to date of death	£700	
Inheritance tax paid on application for probate (see attached sheet)	£54,600	
		£57,505
Net Estate carried to Distribution Account		£324,445

Calculation of inheritance tax in the estate of Mary Blake

Values at date of death	£	£
The Firs	170,000	
less mortgage	65,000	105,000
Stocks and shares (value at death)		263,500
Endowment policy		6,000
Halifax plc	2,500	
Interest to date of death	50	2,550
Yorkshire Bank		600
Premium Bonds		200
Pension arrears		100
House contents		2,000
Car		2,000
Deductions		381,950
Funeral a/c	1,500	
Gas (bill to date of death)	200	
Electricity (ditto)	50	
Income tax (ditto)	700	2,450
Net value of estate for tax		379,500
Tax calculation:		
Net estate	379,500	
Less charitable gifts	1,000	
Less nil band rate	242,000	**136,500**

Tax due: £136,500 x 40% == **£54,600**

Note: the bill is reduced by £2,000 when the house eventually sells for £5,000 less than the valuation.

IN THE ESTATE OF MARY BLAKE DECEASED

Income Account

Dividends received for period from 1 October 2000 to 5 April

Holding	Company	Net dividend
8,000 shares	BT PLC	£800
5,000 shares	Halifax plc	£600
10,000 shares	Powergen plc	£1,500
9,000 shares	Marks & Spencer plc	£385
12,000 shares	GKN plc	£350
Halifax Savings account – final interest		£50
Prudential – interest on payment		£25
Balance transferred to Distribution Account		£3,710

IN THE ESTATE OF MARY BLAKE DECEASED

Distribution Account

Balance transferred from Capital Account		£324,445
Balance transferred from Income Account		£3,710
		£328,155
Less payment of legacies		
Mr David Johnson	£500	
Miss Katya Kropotkin	£500	
The NSPCC	£1,000	£2,000
Net Residuary Estate for distribution		£326,155

MR MATTHEW SEATON

A one half share represented by

a) the contents of the house	£2,000	
b) the balance	£161,077.50	£163,077.50

MISS JANE BLAKE

A one half share represented by

a) the VW Polo	£2,000	
b) the balance	£161,077.50	£163,077.50
		£326,155

Chapter 7

Intestacy in England and Wales

You will find an outline of the statutory rules governing intestacy in England and Wales on pages 11–12. This chapter illustrates how these basic rules affect specific cases. Variations in other parts of the United Kingdom are given in Chapters 8 and 9.

If the deceased left a wife or husband

Case study A

Deceased's family
Wife and three children.

Net estate
Personal effects (that is, strictly, 'personal chattels', including car – unless it was used for business purposes – furniture, clothing, jewellery and all other goods) and £9,500 (in savings bank, savings certificates). The family lived in rented accommodation.

Division of estate under intestacy rules
All to wife, providing she survives her husband by 28 days.

Explanation
The surviving spouse takes the personal effects, no matter how great their value, and the first £125,000 of the rest. In the present example, the net estate is less than £125,000, so everything goes to the surviving spouse and the children get

nothing. No other relatives (for example, parents) are entitled to any part of the estate. It would be the same in the case of a wife dying intestate, leaving a husband surviving her.

Case study B

Deceased's family
Wife and three adult children.

Net estate
Personal effects and £185,000 including investments and value of house which was owned solely by the deceased.

Division of estate under intestacy rules
Wife gets:

- personal effects
- £125,000 plus interest on it at 6 per cent per annum from date of death until payment
- a life interest in £30,000 (that is, the income from £30,000 for the rest of her life).

Each of the three children gets:

- £10,000 immediately
- £10,000 (or part of the fund representing the £10,000) on their mother's death.

Explanation
The intestacy rules give the widow all the personal effects, £125,000 (plus interest at 6 per cent per annum from the date of death to the date of payment) and a life interest in half the remainder. The children share half the remainder immediately and the other half on their mother's death.

If one of the children died before the father leaving children of their own, the grandchildren of the deceased share their parent's proportion of their grandfather's estate. It makes no difference if the widow is not the mother of some or all of the children; where, for instance, their father married a second time. The estate is shared as described between the widow and all the deceased's children. Any children or grand-children under age do not inherit unless and until reaching the age of 18 or getting married. Other relatives (parents of the deceased for instance) get nothing.

This intestacy creates a very difficult situation for the wife if the value of the house is more than £125,000. In such a case, a solicitor should be consulted.

Case study C

Deceased's family
Wife and four children; two of them (A and B) are over 18 years old at the deceased's death, two of them (C and D) are younger.

Net estate
Personal effects and £170,000 made up of £130,000 of invest-ments plus half the value of the house worth £80,000 in total, which was owned as tenants-in-common in equal shares by husband and wife.

Division of estate under intestacy rules
Wife gets:

- personal effects
- £125,000 plus interest on it at 6 per cent per annum from date of death until payment
- a life interest in half the remainder (that is, the income from £22,500 for the rest of her life).

Each of the four children gets:

- £5,625; A and B will receive their sums immediately; the remaining £11,250 is held by the administrators on trust until C and D respectively reach 18
- on their mother's death, a further £5,625 (that is, one quar-ter of the £22,500 which was the mother's life interest).

The administrators must invest the amount so each of the children receives his or her share of the funds representing the £22,500. Depending on the date of their mother's death, this capital sum may be worth considerably more by then. (Remember that all the income has been paid to the mother until her death).

Explanation

The situation is as for case study B, except that, because the wife already owns half the house, only half its value is included in the estate. That is all the deceased owned and the wife may take it as part of her legacy of £125,000. She then becomes the sole and absolute owner. If the house (or the deceased's share of the house) exceeds the amount to which the survivor is entitled under the intestacy rules, she may be able to acquire it by paying the balance to the estate or, providing they are at least 18 years old, by a post-death variation between herself and her children.

Case study D

The situation is as for case study C but the house was owned by husband and wife as joint tenants. Therefore, regardless of the intestacy rules, the wife acquires the rest of the house automatically and becomes the sole owner. The intestacy rules operate on the rest of the estate only.

Division of estate under intestacy rules
Wife gets:

- personal effects
- £125,000 plus interest on it at 6 per cent per annum from date of death until payment
- a life interest in half the remainder (that is, the income from £5,000 for the rest of her life).

The children get

- £1,250 immediately or on reaching age 18. On their mother's death a further £1,250 each (or their equal share of the fund representing their mother's £5,000 life interest).

If the deceased had no children

Case study E

Deceased's family
Husband, mother, no children.

Net estate
Personal effects, £32,000 in investments.

Division of estate under intestacy rules
All to husband.

Explanation
Where there are no children, the surviving spouse gets all the personal effects plus everything else up to £200,000. Mother gets nothing.

Case study F

Deceased's family
Wife, mother and father, two brothers, no children.

Net estate
Personal effects, £225,000 in investments and house in sole name of deceased.

Division of estate under intestacy rules
Wife gets:

- personal effects
- £200,000, plus interest on it at 6 per cent per annum from date of death until payment
- £12,500.

Mother gets:

- £6,250.

Father gets:

- £6,250.

Explanation

The surviving wife or husband gets the personal effects and £200,000, plus interest until payment. The rest is divided in two; the surviving spouse gets one half and the other half is divided equally between the deceased's parents (the brothers get nothing). If only one parent is alive, he or she receives the whole of the parents' £125,000. If he has no parents living, his brothers share that £125,000 equally. The share of any brother or sister who died before the deceased is divided equally between his or her children.

Case study G

Deceased's family

Husband, no children, no parents, no brothers or sisters, no nephews or nieces, no grandparents; one aunt, four cousins.

Net estate

Personal effects, £240,000 in investments.

Division of estate under intestacy rules

All to husband.

Explanation

However large the estate, if, apart from the surviving spouse, there are no parents or any issue of parents and the nearest relations are aunts, uncles, cousins or grandparents, the surviving spouse gets everything.

If the deceased left no wife or husband

Case study H

Deceased's family
No wife, three surviving children, seven grandchildren, two of whom are children of a son who died some years before.

Net estate
£3,500, personal effects to the value of £500; total £4,000.

Division of estate under intestacy rules
- Each of the three surviving children gets £1,000 (× 3 = £3,000).
- Each of the two grandchildren whose father died before the deceased gets £500 (× 2 = £1,000).
- The other grandchildren get nothing.

Explanation
Where there is no wife or husband, the whole estate is shared between the children equally. It makes no difference how big or small the estate is. The share of any child who has already died is shared equally between his or her children; if necessary, this process of taking a deceased parent's share can go on to the third and fourth generation. Any children or grandchildren do not get a share until they are 18 or marry. Until then, the administrators hold the fund for them as trustees.

Case study I

Deceased's family
Two brothers.

Net estate
£3,000 including personal effects.

Division of estate under intestacy rules
£1,500 to each brother.

Explanation

If the parents of a bachelor or a spinster (or widow or widower without descendants) are both dead, the whole estate is shared between brothers and sisters equally. The share of a deceased brother or sister goes to his or her children. If a parent is alive, he or she receives everything and brothers and sisters get nothing. If both parents are alive, they share the estate equally.

Relatives of the whole blood take priority over relatives of the half blood. If, for example, a bachelor whose parents are dead has one brother and one half-brother, the brother gets everything and the half-brother gets nothing. But, if there is no brother of the whole blood, a half-brother receives everything in priority to grandparents, aunts, uncles or cousins. The same applies to other relatives of the half blood: they receive or share the estate only if corresponding relatives of the whole blood (or their descendants) are not alive to inherit a share. An adopted child counts as being a child of the full blood for the purpose of inheritance; so does any illegitimate relative of the deceased. Relatives by marriage do not count.

Case study J

Deceased's family

One aunt, two uncles, three cousins who are children of one deceased uncle, four cousins who are children of one deceased aunt, five cousins who are children of the two living uncles; no children, no parents, no brothers or sisters, no grandparents.

Net estate

£6,000.

Division of estate under intestacy rules

- £1,200 to the aunt and two uncles who are living.
- £400 each to the three cousins who are children of the deceased uncle.

- £300 each to the four cousins who are children of the deceased aunt.

Explanation

The aunt and uncles, as nearest relatives, share the estate equally. But the children of any dead aunt or dead uncle share what the aunt or uncle would have received if he or she had survived long enough. So the estate is divided into five (£6,000 ÷ 5 = £1,200). The dead uncle's one-fifth share is divided into three equal shares for his children (the three cousins on that side of the family). The dead aunt's one-fifth share is divided into four equal shares for the children (the four cousins on that side of the family). The cousins whose relevant parent is still alive get nothing.

It is essential for the administrators to make sure that they are aware of all possible claimants before distributing the estate. They should therefore place the statutory advertisement in the *London Gazette* (and perhaps local newspapers) – see page 171. It is up to anyone who claims to be a relative to prove that he or she is entitled; this is usually done by showing necessary birth, marriage and death certificates. If the administrators have any doubts at all whether the family tree is complete, they should seek legal advice. To guard against the possibility of a remote relative coming forward at a later stage, the only safe course is to pay the money into court or obtain insurance cover. The court can then discharge them from their duties as administrators and any applicant subsequently must apply to the court to prove the claim.

Case study K

Deceased's family

Five second cousins (relatives who have the same great-grandparents as the deceased).

Net estate

£10,000.

Division of estate under intestacy rules
Everything to the Crown (or the Duchy of Cornwall or the Duchy of Lancaster in those areas).

Explanation
Only relatives who can show that they are descendants of (or are) the deceased's grandparents can take a share in the estate of someone who died intestate. To be a descendant of the deceased's great-grandparents is not sufficient and, if there are no nearer relatives, the estate goes to the Crown. It is then called *bona vacantia*. The court makes a distribution of some or even all the net estate, after paying expenses, among those who can show a strong moral claim: where, for example, a distant relative has looked after the deceased for many years or where a void will has been made which would have left everything to a close friend.

This may also happen where the deceased had been living with a woman to whom he was not married. But she is likely to do better by claiming under the Inheritance (Provision for Family and Dependants) Act 1975, since she would count as being someone who 'immediately upon the death of the deceased was being maintained either wholly or partly by the deceased'. This rule has recently been relaxed so that, if the couple have been cohabiting for two years, financial independence does not have to be proved. This gives her a right to claim reasonable provision – probably an income, but perhaps a capital sum as well out of the estate. Such a claim should be made without delay.

The procedure is complicated, and anyone considering making a claim under the Inheritance Act (on an intestacy or also where there was a will) should certainly consult a solicitor before taking any action. It is possible to lodge a notice at court so as to be notified if any grant of probate or letters of administration is made in any particular person's estate and thus have notice when the six months' period starts to run. A solicitor is able to deal with this and advise how to register such a notice. Since action can be taken even before the death of the person concerned, take advice as soon as possible.

Chapter 8

Wills and confirmation in Scotland

Advice on drafting wills in England (see chapter 2) applies equally to wills in Scotland. Use clear and precise language and avoid technical terms and anything not strictly essential. If there is ambiguity or a dispute about the meaning of a provision in a will which cannot be resolved by agreement, the matter may have to go to court, causing expense and delay. Inheritance tax and its exemptions, including the 'seven-year rule' regarding lifetime gifts and gifts with reservation, apply in Scotland. In other ways, there are considerable differences in law, practice and procedure between the Scots law of wills and succession and the law as it applies in England and Wales.

Making your will

Eligibility rules for wills in Scotland are the same as in England and Wales, with one important exception. Children aged twelve or over with their permanent home in Scotland can make valid wills.

I, Mrs JEANNIE SCOTT or DEANS, residing at 999 Waverley Street, Glasgow G43 9ZZ for the settlement of my affairs after my death REVOKE all former testamentary writings made by me and declare this to be my last Will: That is to say I nominate my sister Griselda Scott and Robert Burns, residing at The Cottage, Alloway, Ayrshire and the survivor to be my Executors: And I convey to my Executors the whole estate, heritable and moveable, real and personal which shall belong to me at the time of my death: BUT THAT IN TRUST for the following purposes:-

FIRST   To pay my debts and funeral expenses and the expenses of winding up my estate:

SECOND To give effect to any directions contained in any writings signed by me however informal and that free of tax and without interest unless otherwise stated:

THIRD   To pay as soon as convenient free of tax but without interest the following cash legacies namely (one) to John Lennon, residing at Central Park, New York the sum of One hundred Pounds and (Two) to The Society for the Preservation of Ancient Solicitors the sum of Fifty Pounds (declaring that the receipt of their Treasurer will be a sufficient discharge to my Executors):

FOURTH To deliver to my friend Victor Meldrew, residing care of the BBC free of tax as his own absolute property my oil painting entitled "The Wreck of the Hesperus":

FIFTH   To allow my sister Griselda Scott the free use and enjoyment of my dwellinghouse at 999 Waverley Street aforesaid together with the whole household furniture, furnishings and contents thereof for as long as she may require it subject to a maximum period of two years from my date of death subject to her paying all ordinary maintenance costs, the rates and taxes falling on an owner or occupier in respect thereof and the cost of insurance for reinstatement value against normal risks: AND

SIXTH   To pay, convey and make over the residue of my said estate to my cousins equally among them and the survivors of them all as their respective own absolute property, declaring that the children of any of them who shall predecease me shall take, equally among them if more than one, the share which their parent would have taken had he or she survived me:

Deans

IN WITNESS WHEREOF I have subscribed these presents at Glasgow on 1 April 1999 before this witness:-

Signature of Witness   *DJMcLean*   *JDeans*

Full Name of Witness   Douglas J McLean

Address of Witness   18 Dechmond Street, Parkhead, Glasgow G43 9LK

Occupation of Witness   Mechanic

Notes

In Scotland married women traditionally retained their maiden name and in legal documents this is often reflected. Hence 'Scott' is the deceased's maiden name and 'Deans' not an alias but her married name. 'Jeannie' is probably not the deceased's correct birth certificate name, but is in order in Scotland if this was how she was known.

Various persons are named but their addresses are not given. This is in order only where the person is clearly identified. It is better to give addresses.

The informal writings clause is very convenient to deal with small items. It is acceptable in Scotland.

The cash legacies are unrealistically small. Persons making wills should carefully assess the value of their estate and make a reasonable provision for legatees, who are often close friends.

The provision regarding the house illustrates that clear instructions can be given in a will, even although they may not be bequests of a traditional type.

Every will should contain a bequest of residue to avoid partial intestacy.

The signing docquet is in accordance with current law and practice.

Legal rights

In Scotland, unlike England, you cannot disinherit your husband or wife or descendants completely. Whatever the will says, your husband or wife has a right to a third of your 'moveable estate' – that is, all your possessions except land and buildings. This fraction is increased to one half if you do not leave any descendants. Similarly, the children between them have a right to one third or, if you are a widow/widower when you die, one half of your moveable estate.

A person claiming these rights, known as 'legal rights', simply has to inform the executors. You only have to go to court if the executors refuse to pay. Your surviving spouse or children must choose between their legal rights and what (if anything) they have been left in your will. They cannot have both.

Note: not all items commonly regarded as property form part of a person's estate to be disposed of by a will. Further, such property outside the estate cannot be subject to a claim for legal rights. The most important examples are rights in a pension fund administered by trustees, whether established in connection with employment or personally, and certain types of insurance company bond. If you own either, check the precise legal status of your entitlement and leave appropriate instructions with the trustees as a separate exercise from making your will.

Children's legal capacity

In accordance with the Age of Legal Capacity (Scotland) Act 1991, an individual of 16 or over no longer has a guardian and is legally empowered to give a receipt for and obtain a transfer of money and property. The age of 'majority' remains 18 but this is of much less significance than in the past. There are two main consequences:

First, when drafting a will, refer to an age expressly – 'when she is 18' rather than 'when she comes of age' or 'when she attains the age of majority'. Second, if you prefer the legatee not to acquire control of the legacy until he or she is over 16, you must set up a trust. As there are technical considerations involved, take legal advice.

A will which refers to children is interpreted to include natural and adopted children but not, unless specifically mentioned, stepchildren. Scots law presumes that, if a child is born to you after you have made a will, you would wish to make a new will including the addition to your family. Your existing will may do this by a provision in favour of 'all my children' but, if it does not or where the children to benefit are named, the child born later can apply to the court for the will to be set aside. In these circumstances, the court always does so unless it is satisfied that your real intention was to exclude the child.

Death of beneficiary

A person has to survive the deceased by only an instant in order to inherit. Where it cannot be known who died first, the younger is deemed to have survived the older, except in the case of a husband and wife where simultaneous deaths are assumed. These rules can have unintended consequences so, as in England, it is normal to state a specific period of survivorship of, say, 14 or 30 days.

If the person to whom you leave the legacy dies before you, the legacy lapses. Generally, the lapsed legacy becomes part of either the residue (if it was of specified property) or intestate estate (if it was the residue or a share of the residue). But this general rule may not apply to a legacy to your child, nephew or niece (or one of their descendants) who was alive when you made the will but predeceased you, leaving issue. In this case the issue take the legacy, unless your will says that they should not.

Who should be the executors?

All executors nominated in the will who survive the deceased are entitled to act and unless they decline are 'confirmed' –

that is, officially approved by the sheriff court to administer the will. In all but the simplest estates, it is probably better to have two executors to guard against a sole executor acting incorrectly or becoming incapacitated or dying before completing the administration. There is no rule preventing a beneficiary from being an executor and in many cases, for example wills between husband and wife, this is the best course.

Signing the will

New rules introduced in Scotland relate to the validity of wills dated on or after 1 August 1995. Under these new rules, a will which complies with certain simple requirements (listed below) is now regarded as 'self-proving'. Unless it is challenged – for example, because the deceased did not sign it – the will is presumed to be valid. A will which does not comply has to be proved by a petition to the court, which involves expense and may not succeed. Accordingly, all wills should now meet the formal requirements for self-proving status.

- The document must be signed by the testator at the end.
- If the document consists of more than one sheet, it must be signed on each sheet.
- The signature must be attested by one 'competent' witness, who must sign immediately after the testator signs to acknowledge his or her signature. The witness's name and address should appear in the text of the document or in a 'testing' clause added at the end. This information need not be written by the witness and can be added after the event. Certain people are not competent to act as witnesses, mainly children below the age of 16, blind people (as they cannot see the testator signing) and those suffering from mental incapacity. It is not good practice for a person with an interest (such as a beneficiary) to sign, as this may become material if the will is later challenged. Similarly, a person may, but should not, act as a witness to his or her spouse's signature.

- Blind people may sign their own wills. Alternatively they (and other people who cannot write) may use another method. This involves a solicitor, advocate, sheriff clerk or justice of the peace reading the will to the testator and signing it after receiving the testator's authority to do so. The signature is then witnessed as above.

Storing the will

There is no official depository in Scotland where your will can be kept while you are alive. Keep it in a safe place and leave a note in your personal papers telling your executors where it is. Most solicitors provide safe storage for a will, free of charge.

After a person has died, his or her will is normally produced to the sheriff clerk in connection with an application for confirmation. The clerk keeps a copy in the court books where it can be inspected by members of the public. The executor can also lodge the will in the Registers of Scotland.

Revocation of a will

As in England, a will should contain a clause revoking all former wills. This ensures that the distribution of the estate is regulated by the most recent document. A will is also revoked if it is destroyed on your instructions, even if you are not present to see it done.

In Scotland, unlike England, a person's will is not automatically revoked by his or her subsequent marriage. Unless you make a new will, your husband or wife can only inherit if they claim legal rights (see page 114). Similarly, bequests to a husband or wife are not automatically invalidated by subsequent divorce or separation so, if a marriage breaks down, it is better to put the matter beyond doubt by making a new will without delay.

Co-ownership of property

It is very common for property to be owned in common, usually by two people but sometimes by more than two.

Where money is contained in a joint bank or building society account, it is not necessarily owned in equal shares. There are two main types of joint account. The first requires both the account holders to sign cheques. The second, which is more common, is called an 'either or survivor account'. In this case, either holder can sign cheques while both are alive. On the death of the first holder, the survivor can continue to sign cheques. This type of account, however, regulates only the entitlement of the holder to withdraw and the bank to pay money; it does not determine who owns it. Ownership depends on who put money into the account and their intentions in doing so. Where only one holder put money in and made the account joint so that the other could also sign cheques, the money remains the property of the contributing holder. On the other hand, if the intention was to pool resources, each holder has a half share of the balance. The law assumes pooling resources was not intended, so this has to be proved.

Where both holders contributed, the balance is divided according to the contributions made. If this is difficult to prove, the balance is divided equally.

These rules also apply to joint accounts held by married couples. It is perhaps more likely in the case of a husband and wife that their intention was to pool resources but the presumption against pooling still applies, except in the case of 'housekeeping' accounts which are shared equally unless the couple specifies otherwise.

Where a house is held in common ownership without a survivorship provision (called a 'destination'), each owner's share forms part of his or her estate on death and is dealt with either by the will or the rules of intestacy. The share each owner possesses – usually equal – is stated in the title deed to the property. A survivorship destination usually transfers the share of the first to die to the survivor. In some circumstances, depending on the wording of the title deed, you cannot change the destination. If you are free to revoke it, you must do so expressly in your will. When a marriage breaks down and either the husband or wife is taking over complete ownership, both must sign the transfer documents. This branch of law is complicated and you should get expert help.

Intestate succession

A person who dies without leaving a will is said to die intestate. Where there is a will dealing with only part of the estate, the result is described as partial intestacy. For example, a person may leave a will dealing with his house, furniture and savings, but overlook, say, his life policies. On his death the house, furniture and savings are distributed in accordance with the will, the remainder of his estate by application of the intestacy rules. In general, total or partial intestacy is to be avoided but there may be rare occasions when a person wishes to defeat legal rights claims and uses intestacy deliberately.

In certain circumstances, you can disinherit your children by dying without a will. Provided your estate is not too valuable, your surviving spouse's rights to the house, furniture and cash can swallow up the whole estate, leaving nothing for the children. If you make a will which leaves everything to your husband or wife, your children can claim their legal rights to one third of your moveable estate.

The rules of intestacy are set out in the Succession (Scotland) Act 1964 and represent what Parliament then considered to be a reasonable distribution for the average family. This area of law is likely to be of interest to members of the Scottish Parliament and radical changes may be enacted in future, including changes to the financial limits given here (correct at July 2001).

Under the 1964 Act, the law does not now discriminate between children born in or out of marriage or between natural or adopted children. A divorced person cannot inherit from his or her ex-spouse and, where a divorced person with a child remarries, the child cannot inherit from his or her step-parent. Cohabitees have no rights on intestacy in the estates of their deceased partners. The rules allowing a cohabitee in England to apply to the court for a suitable provision do not apply in Scotland.

In general terms, the division on intestacy depends on the size of the estate, the nature of the assets and which relatives survive. The more straightforward case of a single or widowed person's estate is dealt with first.

Deceased leaves no surviving spouse

When the deceased dies without leaving a surviving spouse, the estate passes to the surviving relatives in the following order: descendants (children, grandchildren and so on); brothers, sisters (and their descendants) and parents; uncles and aunts (and their descendants); grandparents; great-uncles and aunts (and their descendants); great-grandparents and so on until a relative is found to inherit. Different rules apply to different categories of surviving relatives:

Children
The children share the estate equally between them, with descendants of a child who died before the deceased generally taking that child's share. However, if all the children are dead, the grandchildren share the estate equally between them, the descendants of a dead grandchild taking the share that grandchild would have taken had he or she survived.

Children include adopted children but not stepchildren.

Brothers, sisters and parents
Where the deceased leaves no surviving children, his brothers and sisters share the estate equally between them, with the descendants of a brother or sister who died before the deceased generally taking his or her share. However, if all the

brothers and sisters are dead, their children (the deceased's nephews or nieces) share the estate equally between them, the descendants of a dead nephew or niece taking the share he or she would have taken. A child jointly adopted by a couple is treated as a full brother or sister of any other child they adopt or of any child of their marriage. Half-brothers and half-sisters get a share only if there are no full brothers or sisters or their descendants.

Where there are no brothers or sisters or their descendants surviving, the parents inherit the estate equally between them. If only one parent survives, he or she inherits the entire estate. Where there are both brothers and sisters (or their descendants) and a parent or parents left, the estate is divided into two. Each half is further divided as described above.

Uncles and aunts

Next in line are brothers and sisters of the deceased's parents – his or her uncles and aunts. The uncles and aunts share the estate equally between them, with the descendants of an uncle or aunt who died before the deceased generally taking his or her share. However, if all the uncles and aunts are dead, their children (the deceased's cousins) share the estate equally between them, the descendants of a dead cousin taking the share that cousin would have taken.

Grandparents

Next in line are the deceased's grandparents. They share the estate between them or, if there is only one alive, he or she inherits the entire estate.

Remoter relatives

After grandparents come great-uncles and great-aunts or their descendants (namely second cousins and second cousins once removed). The further the search extends for someone to inherit, the more complex the inheritance becomes. Take legal advice.

The Crown

Where the deceased dies without any surviving relatives being traced and debts and funeral expenses have been paid, the estate goes to the Crown's formal representative, the Queen's and Lord Treasurer's Remembrancer. This official advertises for claimants in local newspapers. If no relative claims the estate, the Crown may be prepared to make gifts from the estate to people with a moral but no legal claim to the estate, such as a cohabiting partner or a neighbour who gave substantial help to the deceased without payment.

Deceased leaves a surviving spouse

Briefly, the law provides first for the surviving spouse who has 'prior rights' to part or all of the estate. Next come the legal rights of the surviving spouse and any children. The remainder of the estate (if any) is taken by the nearest relatives.

Prior rights

These comprise rights to the house, its furnishings and a cash sum. Except in the case of larger estates, where intestacy is rare, prior rights often mean that the surviving spouse inherits the entire estate.

The house

The surviving spouse is entitled to the house owned by the deceased, provided:

- it is situated in Scotland
- he or she was ordinarily resident in the house at the date of the deceased's death
- it is not worth more than £130,000.

Where the deceased owned a share of the house, the surviving spouse gets that share, provided it is worth less than £130,000 and the other conditions are satisfied.

The surviving spouse gets £130,000 instead of the house or share of the house if either is worth more than £130,000. If the house is part of a larger property run as a business and it would be disadvantageous to separate the house, the surviving spouse gets the value (up to £130,000) instead of the house. This situation could particularly arise with a farm and farmhouse.

Where the house has a loan secured on it, the surviving spouse receives only the net value – the value of the house less the outstanding balance of the loan. This is so even if the deceased had a life policy to pay off the loan on death.

The furnishings

The surviving spouse is entitled to up to £22,000 of furnishings owned by the deceased. These need not be in a home owned by the deceased. For example, the couple's house may have been rented or belong to the surviving spouse already. Where the deceased's furnishings are worth more than £22,000, the surviving spouse selects items to this value.

Cash sum

If the deceased left no children or other descendants, the surviving spouse gets up to £58,000 but only up to £35,000 otherwise.

Legal rights

These come into play after prior rights have been taken. If there are surviving children, the surviving spouse is entitled to a third of the remaining net moveable estate (estate other than land and buildings). The children share another third between them. If there are no surviving children or other descendants, the surviving spouse's fraction is increased to one half.

Calculating the size of the remaining net moveable estate in order to work out legal rights is complicated. Debts and liabilities of the estate must be set against either land and buildings (the heritable estate) or the moveable estate. While a loan secured over the house is a debt against the heritable estate and the funeral account and ordinary bills are debts against the moveable estate, inheritance tax and administration expenses are apportioned between the heritable and moveable estates depending on their respective values. Finally, where the deceased owned heritable estate apart from the house, the prior rights cash sum of £58,000 (or, where there are children, £35,000) is treated as having been taken partly from the other heritable estate and partly from the moveable estate.

Children normally share the money representing their legal rights equally. Where one of the children dies before the deceased, leaving children, these children – the deceased's grandchildren – share the dead child's share. Where all the children have died, all the grandchildren share equally. A child who renounces his or her legal rights while the deceased is alive does not share, nor can his or her descendants. A child's share can also be affected if the deceased gives him or her a substantial lifetime gift on marriage, for example, or to provide long-term income.

The remainder of the estate

After prior and legal rights have been met, any remainder of the estate goes to the deceased's nearest relatives. The order is children, grandchildren and remoter descendants, then brothers, sisters (or their descendants) and parents. The rules for division between these relatives are the same as where the deceased left no surviving spouse. If the deceased leaves no surviving relatives in the above categories, the surviving spouse inherits the entire estate.

Administering the estate

In Scotland, the persons legally responsible for dealing with an estate are the executors. Unless a will provides otherwise, they are not entitled to be paid for their services but, if they seek help, professional fees are chargeable to the estate. It is inadvisable to attempt the work yourself unless you are confident you have the necessary administrative and financial ability.

Appointment and confirmation of executors

Executors appointed by your will are called executors-nominate. If an executor-nominate does not wish to act, he or she can decline to be confirmed. A simple signed statement to that effect is all that is needed. You cannot decline and nevertheless reserve the right to apply later. If a sole executor-nominate declines, the estate may have to apply to the court for another executor to be appointed. In this case, it is quicker and cheaper for the nominated executor to bring someone else in as co-executor and then decline, leaving the co-executor to be confirmed and act alone. For a person who dies intestate, the court appoints an 'executor-dative'. In this case a member of the family, often the surviving spouse, has to petition the court in the place where the deceased was domiciled for appointment as executor-dative (except for small estates: whose value before deduction of debts does not exceed £25,000). Such petitions are best put in the hands of a solicitor. The court normally handles them within two weeks.

All executors, whether nominate or dative, have to be officially 'confirmed' by the sheriff court before they can start collecting in the estate. However, confirmation of assets is not always needed. The rules for payments of up to £5,000 by organisations such as the Department for National Savings are the same in Scotland as in England and Wales. Confirmation is also unnecessary in the case of property held in common by the deceased and another on a title which contains a survivorship destination. On death, the deceased's share of the property passes to the other automatically, bypassing the executor.

If confirmation is required for even one item, all assets (cash, personal effects, furniture, car and similar items) have to be entered in an inventory for confirmation. They do not need to be professionally valued, however, and may be valued by the executor. Unless the title to the property contains a survivorship destination (when the share is disclosed for tax purposes only), the deceased's share of property held in common with another person must also be confirmed.

First formalities for executors

Executors, whether nominated in the will or appointed by the court, have limited powers before confirmation. In this period, they should confine themselves to safeguarding and investigating the estate. They should not hand over any items to beneficiaries. Any person who interferes with the deceased's property may be held personally liable for all the deceased's debts, however large. This liability of confirmed executors for debts is limited to the overall value of the estate, providing they acted prudently and within their legal authority before confirmation.

If an executor discovers that the estate is insolvent, he or she should not continue with the administration but should take advice immediately from an insolvency adviser such as a Citizens Advice Bureau, an accountant or a solicitor. It may be necessary to petition the court immediately for a trustee to be appointed to administer the estate – otherwise, the executor may become personally liable for the debts.

Confirmation forms

In 2000 new forms, including C1 for confirmation of assets and liabilities, were introduced. They can be downloaded from the Internet and are broadly interactive. Printed copies can be obtained from the Capital Taxes Office or the Commissary Department of the Sheriff Clerks' Office. There are no special forms for lay applicants.

Once you, the executor, have all the information regarding the valuation of the assets in the estate and the deceased's debts, you are ready to fill in the appropriate form for obtaining confirmation. When there is more than one executor, one of them applies on behalf of all. If there is disagreement among the persons entitled to apply, the sheriff can be asked to make a ruling. An executor appointed by the will who does not wish to act must sign a statement to this effect. This accompanies the application for confirmation. Estates under £25,000 before debts are deducted – small estates – have special procedures you use to obtain confirmation.

Procedure with larger estates

If it is likely that there is inheritance tax to pay, the Inland Revenue requires a return on form IHT 200. This applies to estates with a gross value over £210,000 and in cases where there have been lifetime gifts or trusts established by the deceased. The procedure is virtually identical in Scotland and England. Form IHT 200 can be downloaded from the Internet along with detailed guidance.

Since 2000 the steps involved in completing IHT 200 where necessary and applying for confirmation are now quite distinct. This has made the confirmation process simpler than before. Inheritance tax due by the executors must be paid before confirmation is sought. Since the estate's funds are effectively frozen at this stage, ask a bank for temporary overdraft facilities to pay the tax.

Completing form C1

Confirmation

Your name and address	Your reference
Miss Griselda Scott 999 Waverley Street Glasgow G43 9ZZ	
	IR CT reference

About the person who has died

Surname	Title
DEANS (Maiden surname Scott)	Mrs

Forenames	Occupation
Jeannie	Retired heroine

	Date of birth
	1 April 1941

Date of death	Place of death
1 April 2001	999 Waverley Street, Glasgow

Address

999 Waverley Street
Glasgow
G43 9ZZ

Testate/Intestate (delete as appropriate)	Total estate for Confirmation	£ 155,208

Executors

Full name(s) and address(es). If nominate, list in order shown in the will, etc.

Griselda Scott
999 Waverley Street
Glasgow
G43 9ZZ

20	Recorded in the Court Books of the
	along with relative Deeds.

Declaration by

Griselda Scott, residing at 999 Waverley Street, Glasgow G43 9ZZ

1. who declares that the deceased (full name)

Jeannie Scott or Deans

died on the date and at the place shown on page 1

domiciled in

the Sheriffdom of Glasgow and Strathkelvin in Scotland.

2. That I am

the sole surviving executor nominate of the said deceased appointed by a Will of the said deceased dated 1 April 1999 which is produced, docquetted and signed as relative hereto. In the said Will I am designed as "my sister", Robert Burns, who resided at The Cottage, Alloway, Ayrshire, who was also nominated as executor in the said Will, predeceased the said deceased.

3. That I/   have entered or am/are about to enter, upon possession and management of the deceased's estate as Execut   foresaid along with the said

4. That I do not know of any testamentary settlement or writing relating to the disposal of the deceased's estate or any part of the deceased's estate other than that mentioned in paragraph 2.

5. That the Inventory (on pages 3 -   ) is a full and complete Inventory of the

- heritable estate in Scotland belonging to the deceased or the destination of which (s)he had the power to and did evacuate,
- moveable estate of the deceased in Scotland,
- real and personal estate of the deceased in England and Wales and in Northern Ireland,
- estate of the deceased situated elsewhere

including property, other than settled property over which (s)he had and exercised an absolute power of disposal.

6. That confirmation of the estate in Scotland, England and Wales and Northern Ireland amounting in

value to | £ 155,208 | is required

All of which is true to the best of my knowledge and belief

Signature   Date

Griselda Scott   10 May 2001

Warning to Executors

You may be liable to penalties or prosecution if you fail to make full enquiries and to include all property on which Inheritance Tax is payable.

2

Inventory

Inventory of

- the heritable estate in Scotland belonging to the deceased or the destination of which (s)he had power to and did evacuate,

- the moveable estate of the deceased in Scotland

- the real and personal estate of the deceased in England, Wales and Northern Ireland

- the estate of the deceased situated elsewhere

Include property, other than settled property, over which the deceased had and exercised an absolute power of disposal.

List the estate under these headings and in this order

Estate in Scotland (heritable property first)
Estate in England and Wales
Estate in Northern Ireland
Summary for confirmation
Estate elsewhere (say in which country)

Item No	Description	Price of shares	£
	Estate in Scotland Heritable property		
1	Dwellinghouse at 999 Waverley Street, Glasgow G43 9ZZ, registered in the Land Register of Scotland under Title Number GLA 999999999, valued by executor at		65,000
	Moveable property		
2	Household furniture and personal effects, valued by the executor at		2,500
3	Partick Bank plc, 123 Somewhere Street, Glasgow G0 9ZZ on account 123456, interest nil		7,589
4	Wonderful Building Society, PO Box 1, Glasgow G0 1AA on account 1234.98765, and interest £9.50		75,009
5	National Savings Income Bonds £5,000 bonds Interest for 20 days		5,000 20
	Premium Savings Bonds		5
6	Department of Social Security balance on retirement pension		85
7	Summary for Confirmation Heritable Estate in Scotland £65,000 Moveable Estate in Scotland £90,208 Estate in England and Wales nil Estate in Northern Ireland nil Total for Confirmation £155,208 Estate Elsewhere nil		90,208
		Carried forward	

3

Summary of amounts to be paid on this form

Tax and interest being paid now which may not be paid by instalments *(J11 on IHT200)*

Tax and interest being paid now which may be paid by instalments *(J18 on IHT200)*

Tax and interest being paid now on this form *(J19 on IHT200)* £0.00

For IR CT use only

Received this day the sum of

£

for Inheritance Tax and interest thereon

IR CT Cashiers

_____
for Commissioners of Inland Revenue

The stamp and receipt are provisional.
The Inventory will be examined after it has been recorded and the amount of tax adjusted if necessary.

Additional information required for Commissary purposes

Joint property

Was the deceased a "joint owner" of any property Heritable or Moveable passing by survivorship? If so, identify the property, state the share and appropriate reason below.

No ✔ Yes

	Value of share

Descendants surviving the deceased

State the number of any children or grandchildren who survived the deceased

Children: 0   Grandchildren: 0

Aggregate chargeable transfer

Enter the aggregate chargeable transfer *(box H15 on IHT200)* £ 0

Enter the total liabilities at the death £ 0

Is the estate an excepted/small estate? No   Yes ✔

Your telephone number   0141 221 4667

You can obtain form C1 and complete it manually or download an interactive version. At the time of writing, the form cannot be 'saved' on computer systems without the use of additional software. This makes the interactive form difficult to complete unless you have all the information assembled before you start.

You first fill in details of the deceased and the appointment of executors. You have to make formal statements and complete and sign a declaration. Any document referred to, such as the will, should be marked up as relating to the declaration and signed. In the pages of form C1 which follow, you list, asset by asset together with their value, all the estate in the United Kingdom and moveable estate abroad. This ensures that everyone holding an asset hands it over.

Assets should be listed in the following order:

- *Heritable estate (that is, land or buildings) in Scotland.* A typical example is the deceased's house if he or she was sole or part-owner. While the postal address of a house is normally a good enough description, for land you need to use the formal wording in the title deeds. Include the Title Number if the property is registered in the Land Register of Scotland. Do not include here property whose title contains a survivorship destination but use the space later in the form.
- *Moveable estate in Scotland.* This includes cash, furniture and personal effects, car, bank or building society accounts where the branch is in Scotland, National Savings investments and Government stock, shares in Scottish companies, income tax refunds, arrears of pay or pension and all other debts due to the deceased.
- *Real and personal estate in England and Wales.* Real estate (land or buildings) is put first. Personal estate is other types of property, such as shares in English companies.
- *Real and personal estate in Northern Ireland* – as for England and Wales.

Real estate outside the United Kingdom should be listed in a separate will made in the country concerned.

Summary for confirmation

At this point you summarise the value of the estate under the above headings, giving you the total amount for confirmation. There is a set way in which the summary is prepared for the sheriff clerk. *Note*: moveable property outside the United Kingdom such as shares in foreign companies is listed separately.

Lodging the form

You can now lodge the form (usually by post but you can do it personally) with the sheriff court for the place where the deceased was domiciled at the time of death. If you are in any doubt, ask your local sheriff court to advise you. At the same time as you lodge the will, you pay the fee for confirmation. For estates not exceeding £50,000, the fee is currently £74; for estates larger than £50,000 the fee is £105. For an estate with a range of assets, ask for certificates of confirmation for individual items of estate. These cost £3 each if ordered when you apply for confirmation. You can collect the assets simultaneously, using the appropriate certificate of confirmation as evidence of your right to demand and receive them.

After a week or so, if everything is in order, the confirmation is sent to you by post and the will is returned, the court keeping a copy for its records. The confirmation itself is a photocopy of parts of the form you lodged showing details of the deceased, the executors and all the assets of the estate in the United Kingdom together with a page in which the sheriff court 'in Her Majesty's name and authority approves of and confirms' the named executor(s) and 'gives and commits to the said executor(s) full power' in relation to the estate.

Bond of caution

If you are an executor-dative appointed by the court, you are required to supply a guarantee that you will carry out your duties as executor properly before confirmation is issued. This guarantee is called a bond of caution (pronounced 'kayshun') and is usually provided by an insurance company. The premium is around £1.50 per £1,000 and is chargeable against the estate.

Losses caused by your negligence or fraud are made good by the cautioner in the first instance, with the cautioner then seeking to recover the money from you personally. *Note*: insurance companies are generally not keen to act as cautioners to executors who are going to administer an estate – other than small, straightforward ones – without professional assistance. You may have to use a solicitor simply because you cannot obtain caution from an insurance company. Instead of an insurance company, you can in theory have an individual as a cautioner but the court would need to be satisfied that, if called upon to do so, the individual is rich enough to pay the sum due. In practice this course is not an option.

A bond of caution is not required if you are a surviving spouse and you inherit the whole estate by virtue of your prior rights.

Small estates

To reduce the expense of obtaining confirmation, special procedures apply to small estates which, before deduction of debts, have a gross value of less than £25,000. For a small estate with no will, you do not have to petition the court for appointment of an executor and the necessary forms are completed for you by the staff at the sheriff court.

Whether or not a will exists, you apply to any convenient sheriff court by post or in person. You take (or send) to the court:

- a list of all assets and their values
- a list of debts (including the funeral account)
- the deceased's full name and address, date of birth and date and place of death
- the will, if there is one.

The sheriff clerk then prepares the appropriate form for you to sign then and there or to return in a few days' time. The fee for confirmation is payable on signing the form. No fee is charged if the estate does not exceed £5,000. Above that figure, the fee is currently £74. A few days after you have signed the form, confirmation is sent to you by post or to the executor-dative appointed by the court. The will is returned, with the court keeping a copy for its records.

Paying debts

Now that you are confirmed as executor, you first pay the deceased's debts. These fall into three categories.

- *Secured debts*. Examples are a building society loan where the building society has a security on the deceased's home or an overdraft for which the bank holds a life policy as security.
- *Privileged debts*. These include medical and funeral expenses, the cost of obtaining confirmation, value added tax (but not any other tax) due by the deceased and the unpaid wages of any employee of the deceased up to a set maximum per employee. Unless the estate is insolvent, you can pay privileged debts as soon as you have money to do so.
- *Ordinary debts*. All ordinary creditors who claim within a reasonable period, usually taken to be within six months of the deceased's death, are entitled to equal treatment. This means that, until six months have elapsed, you cannot be compelled to pay ordinary debts or distribute any items from the estate. You should use common sense here. If the

estate has plenty of assets and you have no suspicion that there might be large and unpaid debts, you can pay creditors, particularly small tradesmen, as soon as you have the money. Similarly, small bequests (golf clubs or a painting, for example) can safely be made over.

Other creditors

Six months after the date of death or such longer period as executors decide (there is no written rule about this and practice varies among law firms), executors can pay all known creditors and distribute the balance of the estate to the beneficiaries. Creditors who claim later are paid if the executors still have estate in their hands. Executors who have no estate left do not have to pay such creditors out of their own pockets unless it can be claimed they should have known of their existence. Unlike the rest of the United Kingdom, there is no official procedure in Scotland for advertising for other creditors but it is a worthwhile precaution to take.

Problems can arise if the deceased was claiming social security benefits to which he or she was not entitled. The Department of Work and Pensions checks inventories lodged at court and is entitled to claim back any overpayment from an estate. If this is a possibility, the executor should not distribute the estate without having checked the position.

Legal rights

You must not forget about legal rights. You should write to every person who could claim, telling them how much their legal rights are worth and suggesting they take legal advice before deciding what to do.

Children present a particular problem. If they are under 16, they cannot legally decide whether to renounce or claim and, since the surviving spouse has a conflicting interest, he or she cannot renounce on their behalf as guardian. Children aged 16 and 17 can renounce but the court should be asked to ratify their decision. Unless this happens, children can apply to the court later if they feel they renounced wrongly. Where the legal rights are under £5,000, the executors may hand over the money to the surviving parent (or guardian) who should invest it for the children. Alternatively, the executors may open a building society account or buy National Savings certificates in the child's name and hand over the passbook or certificates to the parent. A parent (or guardian) who misappropriates the money may be sued for its return. For sums over £20,000, the executors should contact the Accountant of Court who, after considering the circumstances, decides how the money is to be best managed. The options are:

- a court-appointed manager (for large sums only)
- the Accountant of Court to be manager
- the parent (or guardian) to be manager but supervised by the Accountant of Court.

The executors may contact the Accountant of Court for advice on sums between £5,000 and £20,000.

Transfer of the house

If the title deed contained a survivorship destination, the executor is not involved in transferring the house of the person who died. The deceased's share of the house is automatically transferred to the surviving co-owner. In other cases, the house must be transferred to a beneficiary under the will or the rules of intestacy.

The procedure for this involves, in simple cases, the preparation of a form of transfer attached to the confirmation and, in more complicated cases, a 'disposition' – which is a formal conveyancing document. The documents are lodged in the public registers in Edinburgh. If the titles are already registered, the procedures are different from unregistered property. In either case, take advice from a solicitor. At the same time as the title is transferred, and if money is available, any building society loan can be discharged. Otherwise, arrangements need to be made for the loan to continue under the new owner's name or for a new loan.

Paying legacies

Wills usually provide that no interest is due on a legacy but that it is clear of tax. However, the actual wording must be checked. Otherwise interest at an appropriate rate can be claimed if the executor has delayed unreasonably in paying out. The executor should take care to get a receipt.

Settling the residue

Once the executor has paid the debts and legacies and complied with bequests and any other instructions, the remainder of the estate, the residue, can be divided according to the will. As in England and Wales, the executor should provide the beneficiaries with a draft set of accounts for approval before settling with them. Payment should be made against receipts from them.

Chapter 9

Wills and probate in Northern Ireland

The law on wills and probate in Northern Ireland is similar to that in England and Wales. In fact, the law relating to wills is now almost identical, following the introduction of new legislation on 1 January 1995. This new legislation generally applies to wills made both before and after this date, regardless of when the testator died.

The Administration of Estates Act 1925 does not apply in Northern Ireland. The equivalent legislation is the Administration of Estates Act (Northern Ireland) 1955. Likewise the Trustee Act 2000 does not apply in Northern Ireland. However, a Trustee Bill very similar to the Trustee Act 2000 is currently before the Northern Ireland Assembly.

One major difference between England and Wales and Northern Ireland has been created by the 1995 legislation. In Northern Ireland, provided the will is actually signed after 1 January 1995, a married minor or minors who have been married can now make a valid will. It is not possible for a married minor in England and Wales to make a valid will.

After someone dies and probate has been obtained, anyone can apply to see it or obtain a copy of it at the Probate Office, Royal Courts of Justice (see Chapter 11 for the address). If it is more than five years since the grant was obtained, application should be made to the Public Record Office of Northern Ireland (see Chapter 11 for the address).

Differences between England and Wales and Northern Ireland

Use the basic information already given for England and Wales (see page references below) but take into account the special conditions in Northern Ireland relating to: presumption of simultaneous death of husband and wife; solicitors' fees; an executor not wishing to act; registration of government stock; advertising for creditors; applying for probate forms; inheritance tax payments; form PA1; transfer of a house; registered and unregistered property; distribution on intestacy.

Death of husband and wife

In Northern Ireland, the common law presumption of simultaneous deaths in cases where it is not certain who died first still applies.

Solicitors' fees

There is no recommended scale of fees for solicitors. However, the profession in Northern Ireland tends to follow these guidelines:

- on the first £10,000 of the gross value of the estate – 2½ per cent
- on the next £20,000 – 2 per cent
- on the next £220,000 – 1½ per cent

Where the gross value of the estate includes the principal private dwelling house, the house's value is normally reduced by 50 per cent for the purpose of calculating fees. In addition to these 'standard' fees, the time spent by various members of staff in the solicitor's office is also costed and charged.

Executor not wishing to act

Only if the executor resides outside Northern Ireland or is incapable of managing his or her own affairs and a controller has been appointed by the Office of Care and Protection, can a person named as an executor in a will appoint an attorney. So, when you make your will, make sure that your nominated executors are willing to serve.

Registration of government stock

While many people living in Northern Ireland hold government stock registered on the Bank of England Register, there is also a Bank of Ireland register maintained at the Bank of Ireland (see Chapter 11 for the address). The relevant stock certificate or interest counterfoil indicates whether the stock is registered on the Bank of England or the Bank of Ireland register.

Advertising for creditors

The special procedure for formally advertising for creditors in Northern Ireland requires both an advertisement in the *Belfast Gazette* and an advertisement twice in each of any two daily newspapers printed and published in Northern Ireland. If the assets include land, the advertisements should be in the *Belfast Gazette* and in any two newspapers circulating in the district where the land is situated.

Applying for probate forms

Personal applications should be made to the Probate and Matrimonial Office, Royal Courts of Justice in Belfast or the District Probate Registry in Londonderry (see Chapter 11 for the address). If the deceased had a fixed place of abode within the counties of Fermanagh, Londonderry or Tyrone, application may be made to either address. If the deceased resided elsewhere in Northern Ireland, the application must be made to the Belfast office.

The fees in all applications are based on the net value of the estate. They are:

- net estate under £10,000 – nil
- net estate £10,000–£25,000 – £75

- net estate between £25,000–£40,000 – £145
- net estate between £40,000–£70,000 – £260
- net estate between £70,000–£100,000 – £330
- net estate between £100,000–£200,000 – £410
- for each additional £100,000 thereafter – £65.

The additional fee paid in a personal application is £6 for each £1,000 or part £1,000 of the net estate. Personal applications must be made in person, that is, not by post. The fees are increased from time to time with little prior warning, so it is best to check with the appropriate Probate Office before writing the cheque.

Inheritance tax payments

The cheque for inheritance tax due should be made out to 'Inland Revenue' and the cheque for the Probate Office fees should be made out to 'The Supreme Court Fees Account'.

Form PA1

In Northern Ireland, it is not yet necessary to serve a notice on an executor who is not acting and who has not renounced. It is therefore possible for one executor to obtain probate, without another executor even being aware that he or she is an executor.

Transfer of the house

While property is registered or unregistered as in England and Wales, land law legislation generally in Northern Ireland is very different from that in England and Wales.

Registered property

In the case of registered land, the executors or administrators complete an assent (form 17 – see sample form on pages 147–8). The completed form 17 (see overleaf for instructions on how to complete the form) is then sent to the Land Registers of Northern Ireland in Belfast (for address, see Chapter 11), together with the land certificate, the original grant of probate or letters of administration and form 100A, *Application for Registration* (see sample form on pages 150–1). Both forms 17 and 100A are available from the Land Registers. The fee is £50. If the property is subject to a mortgage, the certificate of charge with the 'vacate' or receipt sealed by the bank or building society should be lodged at the same time, together with an additional fee of £25. Cheques should be made payable to 'DOE General Account'.

Land Registry assent form – instructions for completion

(1) General

Complete all relevant panels and schedules. If the space is insufficient, continuation sheet(s) (size A4) should be securely attached.
Each continuation sheet must be headed with the appropriate folio
number(s) and county, and reference to the panel or schedule to
which it relates. A cross-reference note should also be included in
the panel or schedule (e.g. 'continued on attached sheet').

(2) The deceased

Insert appropriate details and have the Certificate of Identity on
page 4 completed.

(3) The personal representatives

(i)   Insert full name(s) and address(es) and description(s). If the
      details differ from those in the grant include explanatory
      words (*e.g. 'formerly of/known as ...'*). If a name has changed
      or a personal representative has died since the grant, furnish
      appropriate evidence.
(ii) Where there is a claim of executorship, furnish appropriate
      evidence.

(4) Settlements

(i)   The entire panel should be deleted if a settlement has not
      been created.
(ii) The reference to trustees may be deleted if there are no
      trustees of the settlement for the purpose of the Settled Land
      Acts.

(5) The property

(i)   Identify the land or estate as the subject of the Assent. If all the
      land in a folio is being vested in the Assentee(s), this must be
      made clear.
(ii) If part only of the land in a folio is being vested, insert a
      description referring to colours on an attached map.
(iii) The part being vested should be defined on an extract from the
      latest available Ordnance Survey (OS) plan drawn to the

largest published scale. (In cases of a very small plot, or for an area of complex OS detail, the location map must be supplemented by a larger-scale plan.)

(iv) All maps/plans must be securely fastened to the Assent.

(v)   If the Assent deals with two or more separate pieces of land, it may be necessary to number the entries in this column.

(6) The assentee

(i)   Enter the full name(s), postal address(es) in the UK for service of notices and descriptions(s) of the Assentee(s) for entry in the register.

(ii) If an assentee is an existing owner of an estate in the land, or a minor, that fact must be stated.

(7) Assentees' share

If the Assent is to two or more persons who are to hold as tenants in common, that fact must be stated, and the precise fractional shares which pass to each person must also be stated (*e.g. if the Assent is of an undivided half-share to two tenants in common who take equally, the appropriate entry in the 'share' column opposite each person would be 'one-quarter' **not** 'one-half' or 'equal'*). If no shares are specified, any co-assentees will be taken to be joint tenants *inter se*.

(8) Class of ownership

State whether the Assentee is to be registered as 'FULL OWNER' or (where a settlement has been created) as 'LIMITED OWNER' of the land.

(9) The burdens

(i)   Give precise details of the burden.

(ii) Identify which folio or part of a folio and, where necessary, whose estate or interest therein is subject to the burden. (Where the burden does not affect all the Land in this Assent make this clear – *e.g. 'affecting only the land in entry 1 of the First Schedule/the land shown coloured ... on the attached map/the dwelling house on the land in Folio ...').*

(iii) If a burden is a charge for payment of money, identify it as such and state whether interest is payable.

(iv) If two or more burdens are to be registered, their priority *inter se* should be clarified.

(10) Person entitled to burden

Where the burden is a charge or right of residence, maintenance or support, state the name, address in the UK for the service of notices and description of any person entitled to the benefit of the burden.

(11) Execution

Unless witnessed by a solicitor the Assent must be witnessed by two people neither of whom is a party to the Assent. Witnesses must subscribe their names, addresses and descriptions.

(12) Certificate of identity

(i) The relevant details should be completed and the certificate should be signed by the solicitor handling the deceased's estate or, if none, by an independent person having knowledge of the facts.

(ii) Add any other certificate of identity which may be necessary to prove that the personal representative is entitled to make the Assent.

LAND REGISTRY   **FORM 17**

ASSENT BY PERSONAL REPRESENTATIVE

COMPLETE PANELS AS PER ATTACHED INSTRUCTIONS

Note 1

County: XXX	Date: 1 November 2001
All Folio(s) affected:	**Registered Owner(s):**
FOLIO NO. YYY	OONAGH MARY O'BRIEN

Note 2

Deceased Registered Owner: OONAGH MARY O'BRIEN

who died on: 12 MAY 2001

Note 3

The Personal Representative(s) of the said deceased:

1. Patricia Helen Partridge, 3 Lower Street, Belfast – Teacher
2. Norman Bruce Martin, 28 Paul Avenue, Belfast – Radiographer

I/We the above named personal representative(s), for the purpose of administering the estate of the deceased Registered Owner, assent to the vesting of the property described in the First Schedule in the Assentee(s) as set out in the said Schedule and request registration accordingly, subject as appears in the folio(s) and also subject to registration of the burden(s)(if any) set out in the Second Schedule.

Note 4

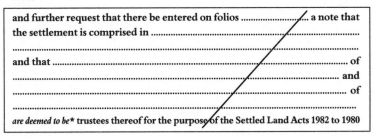

and further request that there be entered on folios ..../... a note that
the settlement is comprised in ....
...
and that .... of
... and
... of
...
are deemed to be ★ **trustees thereof for the purpose of the Settled Land Acts 1982 to 1980**

★ *delete if inappropriate*

THE FIRST SCHEDULE

The Property (Note 5)	The Assentee(s) (Note 6)	Assentees' Share (Note7)	Class of ownership (Note 8)
All the land in Folio YYY County XXX	Peter Morris Eltham Park House Beech Avenue Marbleton Co. Antrim	All	Fee Simple

THE SECOND SCHEDULE

Burdens (Note 9)	Person(s) entitled to benefit of burden (Note 10)
None	None

Note 11

SIGNED SEALED AND DELIVERED
by the said PATRICIA HELEN PARTRIDGE
in the presence of:

SIGNED SEALED AND DELIVERED
by the said NORMAN BRUCE MARTIN
in the presence of:

Certificate of Identity – Note 12

I NORMAN BRUCE MARTIN

of 28 Paul Avenue, Belfast

hereby certify that OONAGH MARY O'BRIEN

named in a Grant of Probate of the Will

issued on 9 July 2001 **is one and the same person as** OONAGH MARY O'BRIEN
the registered owner of the within mentioned folio(s)

Dated this   **day of**   **200**

Signed ....

Application for Registration

Form 100A

Please complete the white boxes on pages 1 & 2 using typescript or BLOCK CAPITALS

For Official Use
Map Ref:

(Left margin, vertical labels: Application Number | Day Code | New Folio Number | Received | NIHE DEV | Mark Off)

1. County: X X X	**2. Queries to be sent and documents returned to:–**
Folio(s) affected	NORMAN BRUCE MARTIN
	28 PAUL AVENUE
	BELFAST
FOLIO No. YYY	
	Postcode_____ DX _____
	Telephone (code) _____
	Fax_____
	Applicant's Land Registry Code_/_/_
If unsufficient space continue on a separate sheet and enter 'See list'	**Applicant's Reference** _/_/_/_/_/_/_/_/_/_/_/_/_/_/

3. Clients PATRICIA HELEN PARTRIDGE AND NORMAN BRUCE MARTIN

4. Fees and Priority (Describe each dealing concisely and indicate whether it affects the **Whole** or **Part** of the Folio.)

List applications in **priority** order	Current Market Value (£)	Fee Paid (£)	Fee Impression
RELEASE OF CHARGE	25,000	25.00	
ASSENT	125,000	50.00	
	Tick if required	**Fee Paid (£)**	
Certificate of Charge			
New Land Certificate (new folio)			
Uncertified Copy Map (new folio)			
Certified Copy Map (new folio)			

I/We enclose a crossed cheque/postal order payable to DOE General Account for

Total Fee	£ 75.00	

For official use only
Fee due £
Fee received
Overpayment refunded ☐
Underpayment requested ☐

5. Documents lodged – list all documents lodged (attach a continuation sheet if necessary)

Date	Document	Parties	Checked
—	FOLIO YYY	LAND CERTIFICATE	
—	CERTIFICATE OF CHARGE	OONAGH MARY O'BRIEN TO BUILDING SOCIETY	
9 JULY 1999	PROBATE	OONAGH MARY O'BRIEN DECEASED	**Date**
	ASSENT	PERS REPS O'BRIEN TO ELTHAM	

6. Special directions
Complete where any document is to be returned to a person or firm **not** mentioned in panel 2.

Description of document _____ NONE _____

Addressee_____

_____

_____

_____Postcode_____

7. Change of address
This panel should be completed if the address of any person named (or to be named) on the folio is to be updated.

Please update the address of _____

to read _____

_____

_____Postcode_____

8. Checklist

a. Have you enclosed the appropriate fee and signed the cheque? ☐

b. Have all deeds been executed dated and witnessed? ☐

c. Have deeds been presented to the Stamp Office or has a PD1 Form ☐ been enclosed?

d. Where the application refers to a map is the map enclosed and does it meet the current requirements? ☐

e. Have all the necessary Land Certificates and Certificates of Charge been lodged? If not have you lodged a request for an order to produce/dispense with production and appropriate fee? ☐

If you have any query about the completion of this form please ring our Customer Information Unit on 01232 251515

9. Declaration by applicant or solicitor

I/We certify that the information supplied is correct.

Signature of applicant or solicitor_____

Date_____

Unregistered property

Unregistered land is in fact registered in the Registry of Deeds, held at the Land Registers. Although no particular form of words is required in order to vest property in a beneficiary, the wording varies both as to whether the title to the property is freehold, 'fee farm grant' or leasehold and as to whether the property has been specifically bequeathed or forms part of the residue. In these cases, ask a solicitor to prepare an assent for unregistered land. The solicitor can arrange for a memorial of the assent to be registered in the Registry of Deeds, for which the Registry charges a fee of £14. The memorial is an extract of the assent giving the date, names of the parties executing the deed, the address of the property and whether the property is freehold or leasehold.

Distribution on intestacy

The main difference between English and Northern Irish law about wills and probate relates to the rules on intestacy. In Northern Ireland, unlike in England and Wales, no life interests are created on intestacy. As in England, the nearest relatives in a fixed order are entitled to apply for the grant of letters of administration and, if the nearest relative does not wish to be administrator, he or she can renounce the right to do so, in favour of the next nearest.

The surviving spouse normally becomes the administrator. Where there is a surviving spouse, he or she is always entitled to the deceased's personal effects, no matter how great their value. If there is only one child, the surviving spouse is entitled to the first £125,000 of the estate. In addition the spouse is entitled to interest at 6 per cent from the date of death to the date of payment and, after payment of all debts and administration expenses, to half the residue. The remaining half share of the residue passes to the child, either absolutely if the child is over 18 or in trust until the child becomes 18.

If there are two or more children, the surviving spouse only receives a third of the residue, with two thirds divided between the remaining children. This rule applies no matter how many children there are.

If there is no surviving spouse, the entire estate is divided equally between the children. If any child has died before the intestate, the children of the deceased child divide their parent's share between them. As in England, no distinction is made between natural or adopted children.

Where someone dies intestate without children but with one or both parents still alive, the surviving spouse (if any) receives the first £200,000 of the estate, plus interest at 6 per cent per annum from the date of death until payment, together with half the residue. The other half of the residue passes to the parents of the intestate equally or, if only one parent is still alive, to that parent in its entirety. If there is no surviving spouse, the parents inherit the entire estate equally or, if only one parent survives, that parent inherits the entire estate.

Where someone dies without children and parents but with brothers or sisters or children of predeceased brothers and sisters, the surviving spouse (if any) takes the first £200,000, plus interest at 6 per cent from the date of death to the date of payment, and half of the residue. The other half of the residue is divided between the surviving brothers and sisters. The children of a predeceased brother or sister divide their parent's share equally between them. If there is no surviving spouse, the entire estate is divided between the brothers and sisters, with the issue of any predeceased brother or sister taking their parent's share.

There is a second major difference between English and Northern Irish law. In Northern Ireland, in the case of there being no issue, parents, siblings, grandparents or uncles or aunts or their issue, there is a special order of precedence to determine the next of kin. Consult a solicitor.

The following examples relate to those given in Chapter 7: 'Intestacy in England and Wales', but assume that the deceased had died while domiciled in Northern Ireland.

Case study A

Deceased's family
Wife and three children.

Net estate
Personal effects (that is, strictly, 'personal chattels', including car unless it was used for business purposes, furniture, clothing, jewellery and all goods and other chattels) and £9,500 (in savings bank and savings certificates). The family lived in rented accommodation.

Division of estate under intestacy rules
All to wife.

Explanation
The entire estate passes to the wife, as the surviving spouse takes the personal effects no matter how great their value and the first £125,000 of the rest of the net estate.

Case study B

Deceased's family
Wife and three adult children.

Net estate
Personal effects and £185,000 including investments and house, owned solely by the deceased husband.

Division of estate under intestacy rules
Wife gets:
- personal effects
- £125,000 plus interest thereon at 6 per cent per annum from the date of death until payment
- £20,000 absolutely.

The three children get £40,000 divided between them equally: i.e. £13,333.33 each.

Explanation

The intestacy rules give the widow all the personal effects, £125,000 (plus interest at 6 per cent from the date of death to the date of payment) and a third of the remainder. The children share the remaining two thirds equally.

If one of the children had died before the father, leaving any children, then those grandchildren of the deceased share their parent's portion of their grandfather's estate. As in England, if the widow is not the mother of some or all of the children it makes no difference.

Case study C

Deceased's family

Wife and four children; two of them are over 18 years old at the deceased's death, two of them are younger.

Net estate

Personal effects and £170,000, made up of £130,000 of investments and half the value of the house, worth £80,000 in total, which was owned as tenants-in-common in equal shares by husband and wife.

Division of estate under intestacy rules

Wife gets:

- personal effects
- £125,000 plus interest at 6 per cent per annum from date of death until payment
- £15,000 absolutely.

The four children receive £30,000 between them: i.e. £7,500 each.

Explanation

The explanation for case study C is similar to that for case study B. As the wife already owns half the house, only the remaining half is distributed. The widow may take it as part of her legacy of £125,000. The administrator invests the money for the two minor children until their respective eighteenth birthdays. During that time, the administrator has discretion to apply some of the income to their maintenance.

Case study D

The situation is as for case study C, but the house was owned by husband and wife as joint tenants. Therefore, regardless of the intestacy rules, the wife acquires the rest of the house automatically and becomes the sole owner. The intestacy rules only apply to the rest of the estate, so the wife gets:

- personal effects
- £125,000 plus interest thereon at 6 per cent per annum from date of death until payment
- £1,666.66 absolutely.

The children divide £3,333.34 between them (i.e. they each receive £833.34 absolutely). There is no life interest under the intestacy rules in Northern Ireland, so the surviving spouse receives a third of the residue, with two-thirds divided between the children.

Case studies E, F, G and H

These are the same in Northern Ireland as in England and Wales.

Case study I

Deceased's family
Two brothers.

Net estate
£3,000 including personal effects.

Division of estate under intestacy rules
£1,500 to each brother.

Explanation
If the parents of a bachelor or a spinster (or widow or widower without descendants) are both dead, the whole estate is shared between brothers and sisters equally. The share of a deceased brother or sister goes to his or her children. If one parent is still alive, he or she gets everything. If both parents are alive, they share the estate equally.

Unlike in England, relatives of the whole blood and the half blood are treated equally in Northern Ireland. If, for example, a bachelor whose parents are dead has one brother and one half-brother, the estate is divided equally between the brother and the half-brother. If there is no brother of the whole blood, a half-brother receives everything in priority to grandparents, or aunts, uncles or cousins. In these complex cases, seek a solicitor's advice.

Case study J

This case study has the same result in Northern Ireland as in England. However, the statutory advertisement should be placed in the *Belfast Gazette* and also on two separate occasions in two different local newspapers.

Case study K

Deceased's family
Five second cousins (relatives who have the same great-grandparents as the deceased).

Net estate
£10,000.

Division of estate under intestacy rules
Each second cousin will receive £2,000.

Explanation
Unlike in England, second cousins inherit and where they are all related in the same degree, they inherit equally.

The legislation concerning possible claims by next of kin is contained in the Inheritance (Provision for Family and Dependants) (Northern Ireland) Order 1977. The legislation is similar to the 1975 English Act. Anyone considering making a claim should consult a solicitor.

Part Three

Help with queries

Chapter 10

Problems with wills

Is the will valid?

Executors responsible for an estate and getting probate for it before distribution to the beneficiaries are strictly regulated by law. They also commonly face problems which can slow progress and can mean, at the worst, that the rules of intestacy apply.

No will can be found

The deceased person may never have made a will but what if one of the family believes that he or she did make one and it cannot be found? If a thorough search of papers and possessions fails to discover the will, one possible step is to write to local firms of solicitors and banks who might have been employed to make or keep a will on the deceased's behalf. If all enquiries fail, the rules of intestacy apply.

Was it signed properly?

The will should be carefully checked to ensure that it has been signed by the testator and that the testator's signature has been witnessed by two witnesses (who must not be beneficiaries to the will). Both witnesses must have been present when the will was signed. As executor, if you have any doubts about the signing of the will, check with the witnesses. If the will has not been properly signed and witnessed, the probate registrar may declare it invalid or at the very least require a sworn affidavit to explain the irregularity.

Was the will dated?

If it is not dated, it is invalid. Sometimes, it is apparent that a will has been changed or that some other document has been attached. Take all the documentation you have to the probate registrar who can advise whether any of it should be counted as part of the will.

Is it the last will?

Even if you find a will which is properly dated and witnessed, it is not necessarily the last will the deceased made. The older the will, the greater the chance that a later will or a codicil exists, changing its terms. Always make further enquiries to be sure. Remember, too, that even an apparently valid will may have been wholly or partly invalidated by a subsequent marriage or divorce.

Problems with the testator

Did the testator have 'testamentary capacity'?

In order to make a valid will, a testator must understand what he or she owns, understand the effect of the will and recognise individuals to whom he or she might have responsibilities – for instance, a wife with young children. As executor, if you believe the testator lacked testamentary capacity, you need medical evidence to support your case and should take legal advice.

Was the testator threatened or improperly influenced?

Anyone wishing to challenge the will on these grounds must show that the testator was induced to make it by force, fear or fraud or that in some other way the will was not made voluntarily. Legal advice should be taken before attempting to challenge a will on these grounds.

If a potential beneficiary decides to challenge the will, he or she applies to the probate registry for a 'caveat'. This prevents an application for probate being made. It covers all registries and lasts for six months. If not renewed, it lapses. While it is in force, probate cannot be issued. As executor, if a caveat has been registered, you first have to resolve the problem with the applicant. If you cannot, you have to issue a warning to the registry which has the effect of beginning an action in the court to settle probate. This is an area requiring specialist knowledge, so seek legal advice at an early stage.

Is the will or distribution on intestacy unfair?

If it is generally agreed by the beneficiaries that the will (or intestacy) has not made reasonable provision for all the interested parties, they can enter into a 'post-death variation'. This has the effect of rewriting the will or intestacy rules. This step must be taken within two years of the death. If the variation reduces the share of a beneficiary who is under 18, the court's approval must be obtained. If you wish to make such an agreement, take legal advice.

If there is no agreement and the matter remains in dispute, the only recourse is to take the dispute to court. Probate actions can be very expensive, in effect transferring a substantial proportion of the estate from the beneficiaries to their solicitors and barristers. If there is no alternative, the claimant has to file a claim no later than six months after the grant of probate or letters of administration. If there is any risk of a claim being made, executors should limit any distribution made during that six-month period. Those entitled to claim under the relevant legislation are:

- the husband or wife of the deceased
- the former husband or wife of the deceased if they have not remarried or relinquished their claim in matrimonial proceedings

- a cohabiting partner of the deceased who has lived with the deceased for at least two years immediately prior to the death
- a child of the deceased
- a person treated as a child of the family by the deceased (this would normally include any stepchildren).
- any other person who was being wholly or partly maintained by the deceased at the date of his or her death.

Having the right to claim does not mean that you automatically win your case if you do claim. Legal costs of the action are a matter for the court to decide.

Other problems with wills

Bankrupt beneficiaries

If you suspect that a beneficiary is bankrupt, you should make further enquiries, including a search on form K16 at the Land Charges Registry. Any payments due to a bankrupt must be made to his or her trustee in bankruptcy who must produce a S.307 notice under the Insolvency Act 1986.

Missing beneficiaries

Use what detective qualities you have. In addition to family networks and newspaper advertisements, a letter to the Department of Work and Pensions in Newcastle may produce a lead. Genealogists can be engaged on a 'no-find no-fee' basis – check that their finding fee is a reasonable proportion of the sum involved.

Problem executors or administrators

If it appears that a personal representative is unsuitable or failing to carry out his or her duties, an application for removal can be made to the High Court. Before doing so, it is wise to ask the Probate Registrar or a solicitor with specific experience for advice.

Claims by ex-spouses

If there is an ex-spouse to whom maintenance is still being paid following a divorce or separation, he or she is entitled to make a claim against the estate, so remember to take this possibility into account. The extent of the claim will depend upon the size of the estate and the other claimants.

Joint property

If two people own a house as joint tenants and one dies, the deceased's share passes automatically to the survivor. But, if they own the house as tenants in common and one dies, the share becomes part of the estate. If the survivor does not wish to sell the house and agreement cannot be reached for the survivor to buy out the estate of the deceased person, the executors have to apply to the Court for an order for sale. This can be tricky if children of the deceased are living in the house. Seek legal advice if this becomes a problem.

Court of Protection

If the affairs of the person who has died have been administered by the Court of Protection (in cases of mental illness, for example), there are formalities to go through with the court before the assets of the deceased can come under the control of the personal representatives. This usually requires the 'receiver' to file final accounts at the Court of Protection but, if all parties agree, that requirement can be waived. The receiver is the person appointed by the court to look after the financial affairs of people who cannot look after themselves, known as 'patients'.

Foreign property

Generally speaking, if a deceased person owned property or land in another country, the laws there determine what happens to the property at death. Seek advice from a solicitor with specific knowledge of the relevant law.

Foreign domicile

If the deceased person had a foreign domicile (i.e. the country which was recognised as his or her permanent home), a different system of law applies to the administration of the estate.

Negligence by executors and administrators

If the administration is being conducted by an executor who is also a solicitor, or if you have instructed a solicitor to deal with the administration for you, he or she is liable at law for negligence. For example, if the solicitor misinterprets the will and pays out to someone who should not have benefited, or if he or she acts in another negligent way, he or she has to pay any money that cannot be recovered. As a solicitor, he or she must hold insurance to cover this possibility. If you are a lay executor, always take advice when a problem crops up which you do not understand. Remember, you may be personally liable if things go wrong. If you act on advice from a solicitor (preferably in writing) and the advice is wrong, the solicitor is liable.

A common oversight is to fail to advertise for debts in the *London Gazette*. If you distribute the estate before realising that the deceased owed money, you may be faced with meeting the debt yourself.

Chapter 11

Useful information

Use this chapter to check the meaning of common legal terms and to find addresses of organisations you need to contact or which can help with specific questions. You will also find a table of tax rates, tax reliefs and fees (all for 2001–2) charged by the Probate Registrar and other bodies.

Glossary of common legal terms

Lay executors need to understand clearly the meaning of legal terminology and expressions used in connection with wills and probate. Some of them are obscure or unusual. Always check if you are uncertain. The most commonly used words and expressions are:

administrator   the person who administers the estate of a person who has died intestate

bequest   a gift of a particular object or cash as opposed to 'devise' which means land or buildings

chattels   personal belongings: for example jewellery, furniture, wine, pictures, books, even cars and horses not used for business. Does *not* include money or investments

child   (referred to in a will or intestacy) child of the deceased including adopted and illegitimate children but, unless specifically included in a will, not stepchildren

co-habitee   a partner of the deceased who may be able to claim a share of the estate. The term 'common law wife' has no legal force

confirmation   the document issued to executors by the sheriff court in Scotland to authorise them to administer the estate

demise   a grant of a lease

devise   a gift of house or land

disposition   a formal conveyancing document in Scotland

estate   all the assets and property of the deceased, including houses, cars, investments, money and personal belongings

executor   the person appointed in the will to administer the estate of a deceased person

heritable estate   land and buildings in Scotland

inheritance tax   the tax which may be payable when the total estate of the deceased person exceeds a set threshold (subject to various exemptions and adjustments)

intestate   a person who dies without making a will

issue   all the descendants of a person, i.e. children, grandchildren, great grandchildren

legacy   a gift of money

minor   a person under 18 years of age

moveable estate   property other than land and buildings in Scotland

next of kin	the person entitled to the estate when a person dies intestate
letters of administration	the document issued to administrators by a probate registry to authorise them to administer the estate of an intestate
personal estate or personalty	all the investments and belongings of a person apart from land and buildings
personal representative	a general term for both administrators and executors
probate of the will	the document issued to executors by a probate registry in England, Wales and Northern Ireland to authorise them to administer the estate
proving the will	making the application for probate to a probate registry
probate registry	the Government Office which deals with probate matters. The Principal Probate Registry is in London with district registries in cities and some large towns
real estate or realty	land and buildings owned by a person
residue	what is left of the estate to share out after all the debts and specific bequests and legacies have been paid
specific bequests	particular items gifted by will. They may be referred to as 'specific legacies'
testator	a person who makes a will
will	the document in which you say what is to happen to your possessions on your death

Useful addresses

For England and Wales plus UK national addresses

Department for National Savings
Glasgow G58 1SB
Use this office for enquiries about Capital Bonds, Children's Bonus Bonds, FIRST Option Bonds, Fixed Rate Savings Bonds, Ordinary Accounts and Investment Accounts

Department for National Savings
Durham DH99 1NS
Enquiries about Deposit Bonds, Cash mini-ISAs, Savings Certificates, SAYE Contracts and Yearly Plan Agreements

Department for National Savings
Blackpool FY3 9YP
Enquiries about Premium bonds, Income bonds, Pensioners' guaranteed bonds
Tel: (0845) 964 5000
Central helpline for enquiries about National Savings products, including advice on filling in form NSA 904 'Death of a Holder of National Savings'
Website: www.nationalsavings.co.uk
Has a facility for customers to e-mail enquiries

Department of Work and Pensions
Newcastle Benefits Directorate
Longbenton
Newcastle upon Tyne NE98 1ZZ
For pensions enquiries
Tel: 0191-213 5000
Website: www.dss.gov.uk

Inland Revenue Capital Taxes Office
Ferrers House
PO Box 38
Castle Meadow Road
Nottingham NG2 1BB
Tel: 0115-974 2400
Inheritance tax helpline

Websites: www.inlandrevenue.gov.uk
Home page with leaflets to download free of charge
www.inlandrevenue.gov.uk/cto/iht.htm
Inheritance tax

The Law Society of England and Wales
113 Chancery Lane
London WC2A 1PL
Tel: (0870) 606 6575
Public information including solicitors who specialise in wills and probate
Tel: (0870) 606 6565 *(helpline)*
Tel: 020-7242 1222 *(head office)*
Website: www.lawsociety.org.uk

London Gazette
PO Box 7923
London SE1 5ZH
Tel: 020-7394 4580

Office for the Supervision of Solicitors
Victoria Court
8 Dormer Place
Leamington Spa
Warwickshire CV32 5AE
Tel: (0845) 608 6565 *(helpline)*
Website: www.solicitors-online.com
Information on solicitors specialising in wills and probate

The Principal Probate Registry
First Avenue House
42–49 High Holborn
London WC1V 6NP
Tel: 020-7947 6939 *(information and advice)*
Tel: 020-7947 7602 *(for the hard of hearing)*
Tel: 020-7947 6983 *(orderline for probate forms and guidance notes)*
Website: www.courtservice.gov.uk

Oyez Straker
Oyez House, 16 Third Avenue
Denbigh West Industrial Estate
Bletchley
Milton Keynes MK1 1TG
Tel: (01908) 361166
Telesales for probate forms and other stationery

The Stationery Office
PO Box 29
St Crispins House
Duke Street
Norwich NR3 1GN
Tel: (0870) 600 5522
Orders for government documents and specialist books
Website: www.clicktso.com

For Scotland

Accountant of Court
2 Parliament Square
Edinburgh EH1 1RQ
Tel: 0131-240 6758
Website: www.scotcourts.gov.uk

Inland Revenue Capital Taxes
Meldrum House
15 Drumsheugh Gardens
Edinburgh EH3 7UG
Tel: 0131-777 4050 or 4060 *(helplines)*
Websites: www.inlandrevenue.gov.uk *(home page with leaflets to download free of charge)*,
www.inlandrevenue.gov.uk/cto/iht.htm *(inheritance tax)*

Law Society of Scotland
26 Drumsheugh Gardens
Edinburgh EH3 7YR
Tel: 0131-226 7411 *(head office) (0870) 5455554*
Recorded information including referral system for local specialist solicitors
Website: www.lawscot.org.uk

Registers of Scotland
Customer Service Centre
Erskine House
68 Queen Street
Edinburgh EH2 4NF

or

Registers of Scotland
Customer Service Centre
9 George Square
Glasgow G2 1DY
Tel: (0845) 6070163
Central number for enquiries and advice; use either office as convenient
Website: www.ros.gov.uk

Sheriff Clerks' Office
Commissary Department
27 Chambers Street
Edinburgh EH1 1LB
Tel: 0131-225 2525
Ask for the commissary department for documents and advice on wills and confirmation

For Northern Ireland

Bank of Ireland
Registration Department
7 Donegall Square North
Belfast BT1 5LU
Tel: 028-9024 4901

Belfast Gazette
The Stationery Office
16 Arthur Street
Belfast BT1 4GD
Tel: 028-9089 5135

Probate and Matrimonial Office
Royal Courts of Justice
PO Box 410
Chichester Street
Belfast BT1 3JF
Tel: 028-9023 5111
Ask for the Probate Office for the booklet: 'Step by step guide to personal probate applications'
or

District Probate Registry
Court House
Bishop Street
Londonderry BT48 7PY
Tel: 028-7126 1832
For people living in Londonderry (Derry), Fermanagh and Tyrone

Inland Revenue Capital Taxes Office
Level 3 Dorchester House
52–58 Great Victoria Street
Belfast BT2 7QL
Tel: 028-9050 5353 *(helpline)*
Websites: www.inlandrevenue.gov.uk *(home page with leaflets to download free of charge)*,
www.inlandrevenue.gov.uk/cto/iht.htm *(inheritance tax)*

Land Registers of Northern Ireland
Lincoln Building
27–45 Great Victoria Street
Belfast BT2 7SL
Tel: 028-9025 1555
Website: www.lrni.gov.uk

Law Society of Northern Ireland
Law Society House
98 Victoria Street
Belfast BT1 3JZ
Tel: 028-9023 1614
Website: www.lawsoc-ni.org

Tax rates, exemptions, reliefs and fees

The figures given below are for 2001–2

INCOME TAX

Individuals:	first £1,520 (after personal allowances)	10%
	£1,521–£28,400	22%
	over £28,400	40%
	dividends unless specifically included in a will	10%
	other savings	20%

CAPITAL GAINS TAX

Annual exemptions are:

* £7,200 for individuals
* £3,600 for trusts
* £7,200 for personal representatives for the year of death and for the two following years.

Once annual income and capital gains exceed £28,400, personal representatives and trusts pay capital gains tax at 34 per cent. The tax is charged on the balance (after deducting allowances and taper relief) as though it was income with a flat rate of 40 per cent.

INHERITANCE TAX

Tax rates

Transfers up to £242,000	nil
Transfers over £242,000	40%

Gifts made within seven years of death (PETs) are generally added to the estate before the inheritance tax liability is calculated. Tapering relief is allowed if the value of the gift exceeds the inheritance tax threshold (nil rate band).

Exemptions

Annual exemption	£3,000
Wedding gift to a child	£5,000
Wedding gift to a grandchild	£2,500
Wedding gift to other relative	£1,000
Transfers between spouses	tax exempt
Gifts to charities	tax exempt
Gifts to political parties	tax exempt
Gifts for national purposes or public benefit	tax exempt
Gifts under £250 – to any number of people	tax exempt
Normal expenditure out of income	tax exempt

Reliefs

Business property relief	reduction in value 50% or 100% depending on asset
Agricultural property relief	reduction in value 50% or 100% depending on asset ownership
Woodland relief	available on the death of the beneficiary of an estate on which inheritance tax has recently been paid

Index

abroad
  permanent residence 16
  property and land abroad 15–16, 28, 32, 166
Accountant of Court (Scotland) 137
accountants 87
accounts
  capital account 89, 90, 95
  distribution account 90, 98
  final accounts preparation 89, 95–8
  income account 90, 97
  introductory memorandum 89
accumulation and maintenance trusts 24
administration of the estate 41–4
  funeral arrangements 42–3
  necessary formalities 41–2
  responsibilities 43–4, 107
  Scotland 125–38
  see also distribution of the estate; executors; letters of administration
Administration of Estates Act 1925 53
Administration of Estates Act (Northern Ireland) 1955 139
Administration of Estates (Small Payments) Act 1965 57
administrators 45, 167

negligence 166
problem administrators 164–5
responsibilities 43
adopted children 106, 115, 120
Age of Legal Capacity (Scotland) Act 1991 114
agricultural land see farms and agricultural land
alterations to a will
  codicils 162
  post-death variations 25–6, 163
annulment of marriage 34
assent
  Form 17 143, 144–9
  Northern Ireland 143–9
  and registered property 143
  and unregistered property 152
assets
  abroad 15–16, 28, 32, 166
  business assets 51
  calling in 85–6
  and form C1 126–7, 128–31, 132–3
  and Form IHT 205 60, 61, 66, 67–70, 71
  household assets 53–4
  joint assets 12, 16–17, 28, 52, 57, 102, 165
  Scotland 132–3
  valuation 47–56

see also gifts; property
attestation clause 33
auctions 54
  informal family auctions 54
aunts/uncles 93, 94, 104, 106–7

bank accounts
  business accounts 48
  current accounts 46–7
  'either or survivor account' 118
  executorship account 47, 90
  freezing 46–7
  'housekeeping' accounts 119
  information for executors,
    provision of 47
  interest-bearing accounts 48
  joint bank accounts 48
  Scotland 118–19
  loan account 47
  in Scotland 118–19
banks
  applications to for repayment of
    assets 85
  loans to meet immediate debts 47
  loans to pay inheritance tax 75
  and share sales 85
Belfast Gazette 141, 157
beneficiaries
  advertising for 92, 107
  bankrupt beneficiaries 24, 164
  claims against executors 87, 92,
    166
  disclaiming a benefit 25, 26
  as executors 116
  missing beneficiaries 164
  naming in will 30
  predeceasing 91–2
    Scotland 115–16
  residuary beneficiaries 26
  substitutions 91
  of trusts 23, 24
  under 18 years of age 25, 28

  as witnesses 33
Benjamin order 92
blind people 33, 117
bona vacantia 108
bond of caution (Scotland) 134
brothers/sisters 93, 104, 105–6
building societies 44
  applications to for repayment of
    assets 85
  see also mortgages
building society accounts 48
businesses 14–15, 51
  bank accounts 48
  business property relief 20, 176
  and inheritance tax 15, 20
  partnerships 15, 48, 51
  private limited companies 15
  run by trustees 31
  sale as going concern 15
  valuation 51

capital gains tax (CGT) 22, 86
  annual exemptions 175
  and the home 22
  and household effects 54
  and lifetime gifts 22
Capital Taxes Office 25, 66, 73, 74,
    75, 89, 91, 127
capital transfer tax (CTT) 18
  see also inheritance tax
cars 46, 54
caveats 163
challenging a will 162–3
  caveats 163
  probate actions 163
  see also claims against the estate
charge certificate 88
charities, gifts to 20
children
  adopted children 106, 115, 120
  age of majority 115

claims against the estate 164
of cohabitees 13
disinheriting 55, 114
guardians 11, 14, 28, 29
illegitimate children 106
and intestacy law 13–14
legacies to
Scotland 124, 136–7
the under-16s (Scotland) 136
the under-18s 87
legal capacity (Scotland) 114–15
making a will 111
and parental responsibility 14
and Scottish law 111
stepchildren 92, 95, 115, 164
trusts for 24
wedding gifts to 20
Children Act 1989 14
claims against the estate 28, 55, 58,
92, 108, 163–4
by children 164
by cohabitees 13, 92, 108, 164
by ex-spouses 55, 163, 165
by spouses 163
statute-barred claims 58
clearance certificate 91
co-ownership
in Scotland 118–19
survivorship destination 119, 126
see also joint tenancy; tenancy-in-
common
codicils 162
cohabitees
children of 13
claims against the estate 13, 92,
108, 164
'common law spouse' 13, 168
and funeral arrangements 42
and intestacy law 13, 95
Scotland 120
confirmation (Scotland) 126–33, 168
bond of caution 134

certificates of confirmation 133
fees 133
first formalities 126
forms 126–7, 128–31, 132–3
inventory 126, 130
lodging the form 133
procedure 126–31
when no confirmation is needed
125–6
Council Tax 86
Court of Protection 165
cousins 104, 106, 107
covenants 88
creditors
advertising for 43, 107, 136, 141,
166
creditor priorities 43–4
Northern Ireland 141
paying off 86–7, 135–6
Scotland 136
taking out letters of
administration 72
Crown, estate passing to the 94, 108

death certificates 41
debts 17, 54–5
advertising for 43, 87, 107, 136,
141, 166
household debts 86
order of payment 43–4
ordinary debts (Scotland) 135–6
payment of 86–7, 135–6
privileged debts (Scotland) 135
secured debts (Scotland) 135
shortfall 43
see also creditors
deeds 88
see also charge certificate
dependants
disinheriting 55, 114
obligations to 163–4
destroying a will 117

devises 87, 168
disabled people and trusts 24
discretionary trusts 17, 24
disinheritance 55, 114
    see also claims against the estate
distribution of the estate 85–98
    according to the will 87, 90–2
    acknowledgements from
        beneficiaries 91
    calling in assets 85–6
    final accounts preparation 89,
        95–8
    on intestacy 92–4, 119–24, 152–8
    Northern Ireland 152–8
    paying the debts 86–7
    Scotland 136–8
    specific legacies and bequests 28,
        29, 87, 169
District Valuer 52, 54
divorce see separation/divorce
domicile 16, 166
Duchy of Cornwall 94, 108
Duchy of Lancaster 94, 108

employers' pension schemes 50
endowment policies 17
estate 168
    accounts 89–90, 95–8
    administration see administration
        of the estate
    distribution see distribution of the
        estate
    heritable estate (Scotland) 123,
        132, 168
    insolvency 43
    moveable estate (Scotland) 114,
        132, 133, 168
    personal estate 132, 169
    real estate 132, 169
    residue see residue
    small estates 57, 127, 134–5
    valuation 47–56

estate duty see inheritance tax
execution see signing the will
executors 11, 28, 168
    administrators 45, 164–5, 166, 167
    appointing 29
    beneficiaries as 116
    claims against 87, 92, 166
    and confirmation 125–6, 127
    death or incapacity 60, 61
    executors-dative (Scotland) 125
    executors-nominate (Scotland)
        125
    expenses 90
    and funeral arrangements 42
    guardians as 14
    instructions for, providing 30
    legacies to 116
    liabilities 87, 92, 166
    negligence 166
    Northern Ireland 141, 142
    not wishing to act 29, 60, 141
    number of 29
    'power reserved' letter 60–1
    preparing for probate 45–56
    problem executors 164–5
    responsibilities 43
    Scotland 116, 125–6
    substitutes 29
    as trustees 29
executorship account 47, 90

family provision 55
    see also claims against the estate
farms and agricultural land 15, 20,
        21, 51
    agricultural property relief 176
    woodland relief 176
Finance Act 1986 18
foreign property and land 15–16, 28,
        32, 166
foreign residence 16, 166
forestry and timber 20, 176

Form 17 143, 144–9
Form 100A 143, 150–1
Form ASI 88
Form C1 126–7, 128–31, 132–3
Form DN1 88
Form IHT 200 61, 66, 73–83, 127
Form IHT 205 60, 61, 66, 67–70, 71
Form IHT 206 60
Form PA1 60–1, 62–6, 142
Form PA3 60
Form PA4 60
funeral arrangements 11, 32, 42–3
funeral expenses 20, 42, 44, 54
    headstones 42, 54
    state assistance with 43
funeral wishes 21–2, 28, 32, 42

gifts
    between spouses 20, 22
    and inheritance tax 18–19, 20,
        22–3, 58
    lifetime gifts 22–3, 55–6
    out of normal expenditure 20
    potentially exempt transfers
        (PETs) 22, 23, 28
    retention of interest or benefit 28
    small gifts 20
    wedding gifts 20
grandchildren 100, 101, 105
grandparents 93, 104
guardians 11, 28
    appointing 14, 29
    as executors 14
    financial provision for 14, 28, 29

heritable estate (Scotland) 124, 132,
    168
heritage property 20
home
    capital gains tax 22
    contents and personal possessions
        53–4, 99

inheritance tax 16–17, 52
    and intestacy rules 94–5
    joint tenancy 16–17, 28, 52, 57,
        102, 165
    mains services 46, 86
    making a gift of 22
    mortgage debt 17, 44, 53, 88
    Northern Ireland 142
    registered property 88
    safeguarding empty properties
        45–6
    sale of 86
    Scotland 119, 122–3
    'surviving spouse exemption' 52
    survivorship destination 119, 126,
        137
    tenancy-in-common 16, 52, 101,
        165
    transferring 86, 87–9
        Northern Ireland 142
        Scotland 137–8
    unregistered property 88–9
    valuation 52–3, 86
home-made wills 27
household and personal goods 53–4,
    99
    auctioning 54
    distribution of 54
    Scotland 123
    valuation of 53–4
husbands see married couples

illegitimacy 106
income tax 55, 175
    accounting to Inland Revenue for
        86
    calculation 55
    rates 175
    rebates 55
    tax returns 86
Inheritance (Provision for Family
        and Dependants) Act 1975 108

Inheritance (Provision for Family and Dependants) (Northern Ireland) Order 1977
Inheritance Tax Act 24, 25
inheritance tax (IHT) 7–8, 18–21, 28, 58, 89, 142, 168
  annual exemption 19–20, 176
  bank loans to pay 75
  and bequests 18
  businesses and 15
  calculation 96
  due date 21
  'excepted estate' threshold 61, 66
  expenditure-out-of-income exemption 20
  and gifts 18–19, 20, 22–3, 58
  and the home 16–17, 52
  and household effects 54
  interest on 21, 75
  lifetime gifts 22, 55–6
  nil-rate band 18, 19
  payment by instalments 21, 74
  'PET' provisions 22, 23, 28
  and property valuation 52
  raising finance to pay 75
  rates 18, 176
  refunds 21
  reliefs 176
  revised assessments 21
  Scotland 127
  seven-year rule 18, 19
  and share sales 21
  taper relief 19
  and variations of a will 25
  see also Forms IHT 200, 205, 206
Inland Revenue
  accounting to 86
  income tax return 86
inquests 42
insurance
  car insurance 46
  of empty properties 46

  indemnity insurance 92
  of trust property 31
  written in trust 28
  see also life insurance
insurance companies as cautioners (Scotland) 134
interest
  on bank accounts 48
  on delayed legacy payments 138
  on inheritance tax 21, 75
intestacy 11–13, 99–109, 168
  cohabitees 13, 95
  distribution on
    England and Wales 92–4, 99–109
    Northern Ireland 152–8
    Scotland 119–24
  examples
    England and Wales 99–109
    Northern Ireland 154–8
    Scotland 120–3
  and funeral costs 42
  and letters of administration 58, 72
  and married couples 12–13
  partial intestacy 119
  separation/divorce and 120, 163
  survival by children 13–14, 93, 94–5, 99–100, 101–2, 103, 105
  survival by parents, brothers and sisters 93, 103, 104, 105–6
  survival by relatives 106–7, 108
  survival by spouse 12–13, 93, 94–5, 99–100, 101, 102, 103–4

jewellery 87
joint tenancy 16–17, 28, 52, 57, 102, 165

kinship and blood relationships 108

land certificate 88

Land Register of Scotland 132
Land Registers of Northern Ireland 143
Land Registry 88
legacies 18, 113, 168
    to children 87, 124, 136–7
    death of beneficiary 30
    disclaimed legacies 25, 26
    to executors 116
    fixed amounts 30
    free-of-tax legacies 18
    insufficient money to pay 44, 87
    interest on late payment 138
    lapsed legacies 115, 330
    pecuniary legacies 87, 113
    proportional payments 44
    receipts 87
    specific items 87, 169
Legal Aid 35
legal rights (Scotland) 114, 123–4, 136–7
legal terminology 167–71
letters of administration 12, 57, 108, 168
    grant of letters of administration 72
    taken out by creditors 72
    those entitled to apply 59, 72
    when and why they are needed 57, 58
    'with will annexed' 58–9, 72
life insurance 49
    endowment policies 17
    submitting claim forms to 49
    written in trust 49
lifetime gifts 22–3, 55–6
    capital gains tax 22
    of a home 22
    inheritance tax 22, 55–6
    PETs 22, 23, 28
    to spouses 22
    to trusts 23

London Gazette 43, 107, 166
London Stock Exchange 49

mail redirection service 46
mains services 46, 86
maintenance payments 55, 165
marriage gifts see wedding presents
marriage, revocation of a will by 29, 33
married couples
    deaths close together/simultaneous deaths 13, 140
    disinheriting 55, 114
    gifts between 20, 22
    and intestacy 12–13, 93, 94–5, 99–100, 101, 102, 103–4
    joint assets 12
    joint or mutual wills 35
    married minors (Northern Ireland) 139
    reciprocal or mirror wills 34–5
medical research, use of body for 22, 32
mental incapacity 34, 165
mortgages 44, 53
    beneficiary's duty to pay 53
    endowment policies 17
    insurance policy to pay 53
    paying off 88
    selling house to repay 17, 44
moveable estate (Scotland) 114, 132, 133, 168

National Savings 48
    repayment claims 48, 85
National Savings Office 48
nephews/nieces 115
Northern Ireland 139–58
    distribution on intestacy 152–8
    Land Registry assent form 143, 144–9
    making a will 139

special conditions 140–3

organ donation 22

paintings 87
parental responsibility 14
partial intestacy 119
pecuniary legacies 87, 113
pensions 50–1
  death benefits 50
  employers' pension schemes 50
  lump-sum benefits 50
  overpayments 50
  personal pension funds 50
  in Scotland 114
  state retirement pension 51
  widow's pension 51
  written in trust 51
personal effects *see* household and
    personal goods
personal estate 132, 169
personal representatives 169
  see also administrators; executors
pet animals 28, 46
political parties, gifts to 20
possessions 11
post-mortems 41–2
'power reserved' letter 60–1
Premium Bonds 48
prior rights (Scotland) 122
probate 41–50, 169
  applying for 57–84
  attending the probate registry
    59–60, 71–2
  fees 71, 72, 142
  grant of probate 84, 108
    copies 72
  Northern Ireland 139–43
  personal representatives *see*
    administrators; executors
  Scotland 111–40
  when no grant is needed 57

  when and why probate is needed
    57–8
  see also administration of the
    estate; distribution of the estate;
    letters of administration
probate forms
  applying for 59
  completing 60–1
  Northern Ireland 141–2
  sample forms 62–70
  sending off 71
  swearing the papers 59, 60, 72
probate oath 72
Probate Registry 7, 59–60, 169
professional advice 8, 12, 22, 27, 166
  see also solicitors
property
  automatic transfer 28, 52, 57, 86,
    137, 165
  capital gains tax 22
  commercial property 53
  foreign property and land 15–16,
    28, 32, 166
  joint tenancy 16–17, 28, 52, 57,
    102, 165
  lifetime gift of 22
  registered property 88
  Northern Ireland 143
  rent-free occupation 18
  Scotland 118–19
  survivorship destination 119, 126,
    137
  tenancy-in-common 16, 52, 101,
    165
  transferring 87–9, 142
  unregistered property 88–9
  Northern Ireland 142
  valuation 52–3, 86
  see also assets; home
proving the will 59–84, 169

Queen's and Lord Treasurer's Remembrancer 122

real estate 132, 169
Register of Registrars 50
registered property 88
    Northern Ireland 143
Registers of Scotland 117
registration of deaths 41
    informants 41
Registry of Births, Deaths and Marriages 41
Registry of Deeds 152
relatives
    of the half blood 93, 94, 106
    tracing 107
residuary beneficiaries 17, 26
residue 17, 30, 169
    disclaimed share of 26
    distribution of 30
    payment of debts from 17
    Scotland 138
    on 'trust for sale' 30
revocation
    by destruction 117
    by marriage 29, 33
    divorce and 118
    in Scotland 117–18

Scotland 111–40
    administering the estate 125–38
    children's legal capacity 114–15
    confirmation 126–33, 168
    intestacy 119–24
    legal rights (inheritance rights) 114, 123–4, 136–7
    making a will 111–19
    settling the residue 138
self-proving (Scotland) 116
separation/divorce
    and intestacy laws 120, 163
    and revocation of a will 34

shares 49–50, 58
    dividend payment counterfoils 49
    electronic shareholding 50
    and inheritance tax 21
    PEPs and ISAs 49
    private companies 50
    sale of 49
    selling through a bank 85
    selling through a broker 85
    share certificates 49–50, 85–6
    share holding counterfoils 49
    tax credits 49
    transferring 85
    unit trusts 50, 86
    valuation 49
Sheriff Clerks' Office 127
sheriff courts 116, 117, 133
signing the will 33, 161–2
    attestation clause 33
    dating 162
    in Scotland 116–17
    signing each page 116
    witnesses 33, 116–17, 161
small estates 57, 127, 134–5
solicitors
    consulting 27, 108–9, 166
    depositing wills with 117
    as executors 166
    fees 35
        Northern Ireland 140
    Legal Aid 35
Solicitors Remuneration Order 1972
sound mind 34
specific gifts under a will 28, 29, 87, 169
state benefits 51, 136
state retirement pension 51
stepchildren 92, 95, 115, 164
Stock Exchange Daily Official List 49
stocks 49, 58
    Northern Ireland 141
    selling and transferring 85

see also shares
storing the will 117
Succession (Scotland) Act 1964 119
surviving spouse exemption 52
survivorship destination 119, 126, 137
survivorship period 115
swearing the probate papers *see* probate oath

taper relief 19
tax credits 49
taxation
 copies of last returns 47, 55
 trusts 23, 24, 25, 94
 see also capital gains tax; income tax; inheritance tax
tenancy-in-common 16, 52, 101, 165
testators 11, 169
 blind testators 33, 117
 illiterate testators 33
 mental incapacity 34, 165
 physically handicapped testators 33
 'testamentary capacity' 34, 162
 threats or improper influence on 162
'trust for sale' 30
Trustee Act 2000 31, 139
trustees
 and declarations 32
 delegation of powers 31
 executors as 29
 expenses 31
 and intestacy 12
 and investments 31, 32
 powers and responsibilities 23, 30–2
 professional trustees 31
 use of income and capital 32
trusts 23–5, 28

accumulation and maintenance trusts 24
advancement of capital 31–2
beneficiaries 23, 24
children and 24, 94
created by a lifetime gift 23
created by a will 23
for disabled beneficiaries 24
discretionary trusts 17, 24
fixed trusts 24
income from 24
investments 31, 32
lifetime gifts to 23
protective trusts 24
settlors 24
taxation 23, 24, 25, 94

unit trusts 50, 86
unmarried people
 and intestacy law 105–6
 see also cohabitees
unregistered property 88–9
 Northern Ireland 152

valuation of an estate 47–56
 building society accounts 48
 businesses 51
 commercial property 53
 debts 54–5
 documents, letters and receipts 47
 farms 51
 house contents and personal possessions 53–4
 income tax 55
 interest-bearing accounts 48
 joint bank accounts 48
 life insurance 48
 lifetime gifts 55–6
 matrimonial liabilities 55
 National Savings 48
 pensions 50–1
 professional valuations 53, 54

residential property 52–3
state benefits 51
stocks and shares 49–50
unit trusts 50
variation of the will 25–6, 163

wedding presents 20
widow(er)s
    and intestacy law 12–13, 93, 94–5,
        99–100, 101, 102, 103–4
    pensions 51
wills 11–37, 169
    attestation clause 33
    check list of assets and liabilities
        27–9
    clarity of language and expression
        29
    codicils 162
    in contemplation of marriage 29,
        34
    costs 35
    essential formalities 33
    executors *see* executors
    home-made will 27

invalid wills 162
joint or mutual wills 35
Legal Aid for advice and assistance
    35
legal terminology 167–71
missing wills 161
Northern Ireland 139
post-death variations 25–6, 163
reasons for making a will 11–26
reciprocal or mirror wills 34–5
revocation of earlier wills 29, 33–4
safekeeping 117
in Scotland 111–19
self-proving (Scotland) 116
setting out 29–30
signing 33, 161–2
specimen wills 36–7, 112–13
using a solicitor 27
valid wills 34
witnesses 33
    Scotland 117–18
    signing the will 33, 116–17
    those ineligible to be 117
wives *see* married couples

What to Do When Someone Dies

For many people, the first experience of making the sorts of arrangements that are necessary following a death comes only when they have been bereaved and least feel like finding out what needs to be done. *What to Do When Someone Dies* guides readers through the process practically, sympathetically and informatively. The book covers:

- how to register a death
- the role of the coroner
- choosing between burial and cremation
- how to claim any state benefits that may be due
- arranging a funeral without a funeral director
- humanist and other non-Christian funerals
- organ donation
- arranging your own funeral if you want to plan ahead
- how to cope with bereavement and work through grief.

The book covers the law and practice in England and Wales and highlights in separate sections the important differences which apply in Scotland. A list of useful addresses is also included.

Paperback   216 x 135mm   176 pages   £9.99

Available from bookshops, and by post from
Which?, Dept TAZM, Castlemead,
Gascoyne Way, Hertford X, SG14 1LH
or phone FREE on (0800) 252100
quoting Dept TAZM and your credit card details

Make Your Own Will

If you die without leaving a will, your property may go to people you would prefer not to have it. And, just as galling, the Inland Revenue may end up taking a larger slice of your wealth than if you had taken control of your affairs.

This Pack takes you through the various stages in drawing up a will, explaining in plain English what to do and highlighting some of the pitfalls to avoid.

Inside the Pack you will find:

- step-by-step guidance on how to work out what you want in your will
- four different kinds of will form, with advice on choosing the one that is appropriate for your needs (or on whether you should get your will drawn up professionally)
- tips on choosing executors and on making proper plans to pay minimal inheritance tax
- advice on amending your will at a later date.

The pack is based on the law as it applies in England and Wales and is not suitable for people living in Scotland or Northern Ireland.

Paperback 234 x 155mm
28 pages plus forms & worksheets £10.99

Available from bookshops, and by post from
Which?, Dept TAZM, Castlemead,
Gascoyne Way, Hertford X, SG14 1LH
or phone FREE on (0800) 252100
quoting Dept TAZM and your credit card details